THE AGE OF THE
GLADIATORS

THE AGE OF THE
GLADIATORS
SAVAGERY & SPECTACLE
IN ANCIENT ROME

RUPERT MATTHEWS

ARCTURUS

Arcturus Publishing Ltd
26/27 Bickels Yard
151–153 Bermondsey Street
London SE1 3HA

Published in association with
foulsham
W. Foulsham & Co. Ltd,
The Publishing House, Bennetts Close, Cippenham,
Slough, Berkshire SL1 5AP England

ISBN 0-572-02923-3

Cover and book typography by Alex Ingr
Cover image: *Pollice Verso* (1872) by Jean Leon Gerome, Phoenix Art
Museum, Arizona, USA/Bridgeman Art Library

Printed in China

· CONTENTS ·

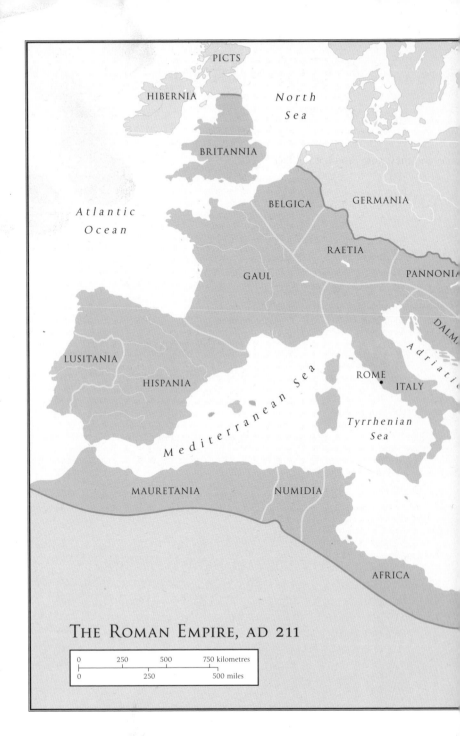

PICTS

HIBERNIA

North Sea

BRITANNIA

Atlantic Ocean

BELGICA

GERMANIA

RAETIA

GAUL

PANNONIA

DALM

Adriatic

LUSITANIA

HISPANIA

Mediterranean Sea

ROME

ITALY

Tyrrhenian Sea

MAURETANIA

NUMIDIA

AFRICA

THE ROMAN EMPIRE, AD 211

0	250	500	750 kilometres
0		250	500 miles

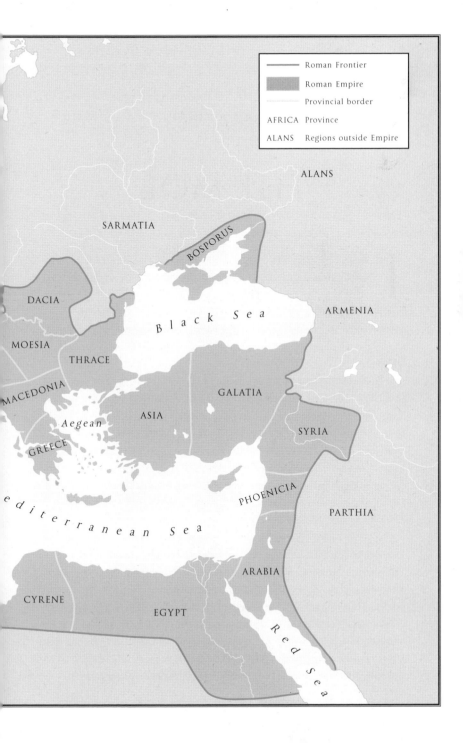

˒ THE MOB ˒

I T WAS THE GREATEST CITY ON EARTH. And it ruled the world. A million people lived in Rome, leading their lives among the vast marble temples and in the narrow, crowded streets. Every occupation known to humanity was represented here, from ditch-digging slaves to craftsmen in exquisite gold. There were men so poor they starved in the midst of plenty and men so rich even they could not count their wealth.

And dominating it all were the twin attractions of 'Bread and Circuses'. Free food came most often in the form of bread on a regular basis, but there were times when roast meats were on offer and a bewildering variety of soups, stews and salads. Even larks' tongues and peacocks' brains were served with no charge. The free entertainments came in even more splendid variety. Nothing could compare to the chariot racing in popularity and excitement. Nothing, except the bloody spectacles of the arena where men, women and wild beasts killed and were killed in savage, bloody combat.

Never in history has a city's citizens been given so much free food and free entertainment. Nor has the fun been so bloody, violent and vicious. The greatest buildings in Rome were dedicated to the slaughter and entertainments. The vast amphitheatre was the largest building of its time, an engineering marvel that drew crowds just to stare. The walls and staircases were decorated with sculptures and murals that would have been admired in a royal palace. Giant obelisks were dragged all the way from Egypt to adorn the chariot race tracks. The theatres were constructed so carefully that the acoustics were not bettered for over 1,500 years.

This was Rome, a city of bloodshed and laughter, of food and starvation. But why was so much wealth, time and trouble lavished on free entertainments and food? Why was Rome the city of Bread and Circuses? The answer lies in Rome's history and her society.

In 510 BC the Romans evicted their king and established a republic. All free men became citizens of Rome, and they were proud of the fact. Unlike inhabitants of neighbouring cities, the Romans did not follow the commands of a king or a tyrant. Each year they elected their own government officials, magistrates and generals. They lived in a democracy, but it was a very strange kind of democracy to modern eyes. The Romans had their own unique ideas about citizenship, its rights and its duties.

Citizens had to be men and needed to be free both of slavery and of various religious transgressions. Women were ineligible for citizenship, though they could own property and engage in business. Foreigners were also able to live in Rome and to make business deals with the full protection of Roman law, but they were not citizens. Alongside the foreigners were a host of free men, mostly former slaves or the descendants of slaves, who might be native Romans or foreigners but who were not citizens. Slaves, of course, were mere property and had few personal rights, none of which affected public life.

In the course of day to day life, these distinctions of legal status were not always clear. A citizen might run a butcher's shop next door to a freeman engaged in the same trade. Even a slave might run a shop on behalf of his master, keeping a share of profits for himself. Only when it came time for elections or if a man fell foul of the law did the legal distinctions come into play. And at that point they could be crucial. A citizen not only had an inbuilt edge in court, but he was spared the worst punishments.

At first citizenship was restricted to free men who could prove a Roman ancestry untainted by slavery or sacrilege. As time passed, however, the numbers of citizens grew enormously. During the fifth and fourth centuries BC, several nearby cities joined Rome in an alliance known as the Latin League. By 300 BC several of these cities had given up their independent status and their citizens became citizens of Rome. By the late second century BC the other cities of Italy, all now allied to or defeated by Rome, began lobbying for their citizens to become Roman citizens. After a short war in 90 BC, this privilege was extended to most Italian citizens.

Nor was the citizenship of Rome extended only to citizens of other states and cities. Free men could be granted citizenship as a reward for service in the army or the bureaucracy. Even outright foreigners could become citizens as a reward for service to the Roman state.

A key feature in Roman concepts of citizenship was that all citizens were equal in dignity and honour, concepts known as 'virtue' to the Romans, no matter how rich or poor they might be. When in a public place any citizen could address another by name and stop him for a chat. Citizens could reasonably expect their fellow citizens to know their names and be polite enough to stop when greeted, even if only for a few seconds to remark on the weather. In the early decades when only a few hundred citizens lived in Rome, most recognized each other by sight and knew at least the family name of anyone they were likely to meet.

Later, as the numbers of citizens rose dramatically, it was impossible for anyone to know all his fellow citizens by sight, but it remained a cardinal insult to forget the name of a citizen once you had been introduced. Rich businessmen and aspiring politicians took to hiring secretaries whose sole job was to follow them about and remind them of people's names.

This is not to mean that all citizens were equal. Apart from the obvious disparities of wealth, there were three distinct classes of citizenship. The most senior class were the patricians, originally a small circle of less than thirty families. These families were all able to trace their ancestors back to the days of the Kings of Rome through an unbroken chain of citizens. Some families could trace their ancestry back to the gods. The patricians alone had the right to sit in the Senate of Rome and to stand for the higher political posts. Noble ancestry was not enough, however, as candidates had to demonstrate they had a personal wealth of one million sestertii before taking office: his at a time when the weekly wage for a craftsmen would be a few dozen sestertii.

The Patrician families themselves were far from equal, and not merely in terms of wealth. In the century to 100 BC about one third of all senior public offices were held by the members of just eight families. And differences in wealth could be huge. Julius Caesar came from one of the most senior patrician families, tracing his ancestry back to the goddess Venus, but was so poor as a young man that many thought he would be unable to enter public life.

Membership of the patrician class was at first limited to the descendants of patricians, but this could be an elastic concept. More than one family which found itself without male heirs would marry a daughter or niece to some talented citizen from the lower ranks and then adopt this man as a son. Thus the family could continue. After about AD 30, the empire's needs for talented administrators led to outstanding citizens, men of talent, being elevated to patrician status.

Below the patricians came the *equites*, a term usually translated as 'knights'. Membership of this class was more fluid as it relied more on wealth than on ancestry. Any citizen with a private fortune of 400,000 sestertii could become a knight and thus be eligible to stand for a range of less important public offices.

The vast mass of citizens were the plebeians, men with less wealth – or none at all. These men might be poor, some lived in conditions of crushing poverty, but all were proud to be Roman citizens and considered themselves clearly superior to the citizens of other cities or states and infinitely better than those poor humans who lived under the autocratic rule of foreign kings.

At first the plebeians were ineligible to stand for public office themselves, but this changed in 493 BC when the office of Tribune Plebis was created. Election as Tribune of the People was open only to plebeians by plebeians. Those elected then had the duty of protecting the status of the people. They inspected all new laws to ensure the basic rights of the plebeians were not infringed and had the power to arrest other public officials if there was any attempt to disturb the peace of the city. It was not only illegal, but also sacrilegious, to lay violent hands on any of these Tribunes. Later still other offices were opened to the plebeians.

Central to the Roman concept of citizenship was the vote. Each citizen had one vote in each election, and they could cast it as they wished. The actual system of voting was extremely complicated, with different electoral districts or classes of citizen electing different officials, but essentially every citizen had one vote. And that vote was a marketable commodity. It could be bought and sold quite openly and without any loss of 'virtue'. Less admirable was armed intimidation or the staging of riots, both of which were fairly common in Republican Rome.

This violence grew increasingly worse during the second century BC as economic problems conspired to make the patricians and equites increasingly wealthy while the plebeians grew poorer. Two patrician brothers, Tiberius and Gaius Gracchus believed the problem could be alleviated by dividing up the vast estates of rich men who used slave labour to farm them. The land, they suggested, could then be rented to citizen smallholders. In 133 BC Tiberius was murdered by his political rivals and in 121 BC his brother was cut down in the course of a riot which claimed 3,000 lives.

Most electoral corruption was, however, less blatant. One of the bonds that held Roman society together was the relationship between client and patron. This came in a wide variety of forms and guises, but all were based on the mutual exchange of favours and benefits. At its crudest a patron would pay his client a regular cash retainer. In return the client would vote as his patron instructed, turn out for demonstrations in support of the patron's favoured candidate or go round writing graffitti in public places. In modern terms, this might be viewed as a part time job, but the Romans saw it merely as an exchange of favours between free citizens.

Very often the client-patron relationship was more subtle. A butcher who sold most of his meat to the household of a rich man would feel obliged, come election time, to vote as the rich man told him. Many contracts to supply goods and services were awarded to clients in return for their vote or their presence at a demonstration. Rarely were these conditions ever specified, but the exchange of favours was implicit in many business deals between citizens.

Even social life could be affected. When a man held a party he would invite not just his formal guests, but also a number of clients. When the official guests had enjoyed their fill of a dish, it would be taken to the clients' table to be finished off. Thus poor men would dine on dishes and drink fine wines that they could never ordinarily afford. Even the guests would bring their clients along. Clients attending with one patron to enjoy the favours of another were known as 'shadows'.

The client-patron relationship affected the working of the Roman state. If a patron was elected to political office his clients could look forward to gaining some lucrative government contracts, as well as invitations to socially prestigious events. The Romans saw nothing wrong or corrupt in a politician handing out public contracts to his clients, or entertaining them in this way. It was simply how their political system worked.

Nor, indeed, was there thought to be anything wrong with a politician using his public office to acquire wealth for himself. The political posts within the Roman Republic were unpaid, but the scope for gaining money by awarding public contracts was enormous. There were limits, of course. The works had to be properly completed and justice was not to be denied to any citizen, but this still left plenty of scope for the enterprising politician to acquire a fortune.

There was another way for an aspiring politician to win votes. That was to circumvent the roles of clientage by appealing directly to the mass of the plebeian electorate. Soldiers such as Gnaeus Pompey could gain popularity by defeating barbarian enemies and bringing glory and loot to Rome. Others courted popularity by showering gifts and promises on the voting public of Rome. Free food and free entertainments were always vote winners. Patricians would vie with each other to provide better and more impressive shows for the citizens. It was this desire to please the public that led to the growth of the games. Some men built their entire careers on their ability to win votes in this way, others bankrupted themselves with the scale of their games. As political weapons, a good show and a sumptuous meal were impossible to beat. And the stakes were high. It was worth spending a fortune to gain public office.

After a series of civil wars, the Republic came to an end in 27 BC when sixty years of internal warfare and murderous rioting was brought to an end by the military victory of Octavian Caesar, nephew of Julius Caesar. Unlike his uncle and other politicians, Octavian did not aspire to be a dictator of Rome. Instead he took up the position of patron to the entire Roman world, gathering all the powers to grant favours into his own hands. Elections were still fought, but Octavian told his vast array of clients whom to vote for and, usually, got his way. Men could prosper in public life only if they were the reliable clients of Octavian. From time to time, Octavian took public office for himself if a crisis needed his personal attention or if he could not find a candidate he trusted. But most of the time he remained a private citizen.

Octavian claimed to have restored the republican constitution, though in fact he was organizing a system of government by patronage. Those who thought carefully about what he had done called Octavian *princeps*, meaning 'most important citizen'. He himself preferred two other titles, both conferred on him by the Senate of Rome. The first, Augustus, meaning 'most worthy', has become the name by which he is known to history. The second, an honourary title given to victorious generals, has come to signify the dominating position he occupied in Roman government. The title was: Emperor.

As Emperor, Augustus could not allow any other politician to gain the means to acquire a great popular following. With all the traditional machinery of patronage in his own hands he had already ensured that only his clients could hope for a career in government. Next he moved to make certain that nobody could get around the client system by appealing directly to the voters. The games, the greatest tools of forming public opinion known to the Romans, became the exclusive preserve of the Emperors.

By taking the games under Imperial control, Augustus set them on the road to acquiring a breathtaking scale and magnificence. A few years later the poet Juvenal complained that 'The people of Rome formerly elected officials and judges to rule the state. Now they long eagerly for just two things: bread and circuses.' He was right. Rome was about to become as never before the city of Bread and Circuses.

PART I
ARENAS OF BLOOD

I

ꞏ THE ORIGIN OF THE ꞏ GAMES

T HE GAMES WERE VICIOUS, violent and frequently vindictive. Hundreds of thousands of men and women died in the arena for the amusement of the mob and the ambitions of politicians.

Some of the victims who died on the sands of the amphitheatres were murderers and brigands, sentenced to death for their crimes. Others were prisoners of war or rebellious subjects of Rome sent to their deaths to provide an example to others who might be tempted to defy the might of Rome. But many of the dead were gladiators, men or women set to fight each other for the entertainment of the crowd. Thousands of these gladiators died each year, the death toll rising as each new politician or emperor tried to outdo the one before in the magnificence of the games in the arena.

The idea of setting men to fight and kill each other for the entertainment of the crowd is so brutal and bizarre that it is difficult to imagine how the bloody gladiatorial games began. In fact, the Romans had a very different attitude to these events than is often thought. The gory events of the arena were certainly entertainments, and were much appreciated for that, but in essence they were religious events which dated back to a time so ancient that the Romans themselves had largely forgotten their origins.

The gladiatorial fights were known to the Romans as *munus*, or *munera* in the plural, meaning an 'obligation' and in particular an obligation to the dead. They formed part of the funeral celebrations with which the living celebrated the life of a member of their family. The idea of gladiatorial contests as part of the munus owed to a deceased relative did not originate in Rome, though it was the Romans who developed the combats to the highest degree.

The Romans themselves thought the idea of the munera came from the Etruscans. These highly civilized people occupied the area north of Rome, giving their name to modern Tuscany which covers a large part of what was the Etruscan homeland. The Etruscans were living in sophisticated cities when Rome was a collection of wooden huts and their culture dominated central Italy for centuries. Cultured they may have been, but the Etruscans could also be brutal. It was their custom to sacrifice prisoners of war at the funerals of leading warriors killed in battle.

However, this form of human sacrifice was not particularly rare in the ancient world. In the *Illiad*, Homer records that Achilles sacrificed twelve Trojans at the funeral of his warrior-friend Patroclus. Homer has Achilles say 'Farewell, Patroclus, even in the house of Hades. I am now doing all that I have promised you. Twelve brave sons of noble Trojans shall the flames consume along with yourself.' Achilles goes on to slaughter sheep, oxen and horses as well, throwing their bodies on the funeral pyre.

Homer, Achilles and Patroclus were all Greeks living before the time of written histories, their exploits recorded in legend. Greeks from that same culture settled extensively in southern Italy, founding cities known today as Naples, Taranto, Syracuse and Pompeii. This area of southern Italy occupied by the Greeks was known as Campania. It seems from archaeological finds that it was in Campania that the habit of sacrificing humans as part of the funeral rites was altered to the staging of fights between potential sacrificial victims. There are no detailed written records of the activities of gladiators at this period, so it is impossible to know whether the change was made to give one victim the chance to escape alive, to provide entertainment for the funeral guests or for obscure religious reasons.

What is clear is that by the time gladiatorial contests feature in written history, Campania is widely recognized as the place where the best fighters are trained. Archaeological digs have shown that the gladiatorial schools of Campania were larger and more sophisticated than those elsewhere. Though it cannot be proved, it is highly likely that the idea of these bloodstained combats originated in the Greek areas of southern Italy.

The first gladiatorial fight to take place in Rome was held in 264 BC as part of the munus owed to Decimus Junius Brutus by his two sons. In his will the dead man had left his sons a generous sum of money set aside to pay for the funeral and six slaves, who were to fight in pairs to the death as a munus. The munus took place in the cattle market, the Forum Boarium, probably on the ninth day after the death when the religious services surrounding the funeral came to an end.

The object of such munera at this time was twofold. The details of the dead man's will had to be carried out properly to ensure the spirit could progress to the Underworld. In part this was because any dutiful son would naturally want to ensure his father achieved eternal rest. More darkly, if any element of the will was ignored, the dead man's ghost might have returned to bring bad luck and retribution to his heirs who had failed in their duty.

The second purpose of the munera was to impress on the rest of society the importance of the dead man and of his family. Children who laid on an impressive funeral for their dead could be assured that their fellow citizens would recognize the wealth and standing of the family. This would have benefits in business and politics. Men who left instructions for a spectacular munus were doing their heirs a favour, though it might cost them a lot of money.

In Rome in 264 BC few families were wealthier or more respected than that of Brutus. Two centuries earlier it had been Lucius Junius Brutus who had organized the coup that ousted the tyrannical king Tarquin the Proud. This ancestor of Decimus Junius Brutus had gone on to be elected the first Consul of Rome, the highest political post in the new Republic, and to acquire great wealth. Any fashion set by the Brutus family was likely to be copied by others.

At first the inclusion of gladiatorial fights as part of the munera remained rare – the provision of free food and drink to all comers being more popular. Nevertheless, those patrician families which did include gladiators in the munera were eager to be seen to outdo the spectacles at previous funerals, usually those held by political rivals. Thirty years after the first gladiatorial games, in 216 BC, twenty-five pairs of gladiators were put to fight each other.

In 174 BC the hugely popular and successful general Titus Quinctius Flaminius died, leaving a will which set a new fashion for the games. His munera lasted for three days and involved no less than seventy-four gladiatorial combats. For the first time the gladiators had overtaken the feasting as the key element of a funeral. These games were probably the first to be held, not at the time of the funeral, but at the festival of Saturnalia in December when the citizens could be guaranteed not to be at work, and so free to be impressed by the spectacle.

These early munera were held in the Forum Boarium for a number of reasons. The first was the fact that the open, rectangular space which was usually occupied by cattle stalls, could be easily cleared to provide a large fighting area. The second was that the shops and temples which lined the market provided convenient seating and standing spaces for the citizens drawn to watch the events. A few enterprising shopkeepers rented out their upper windows to spectators, but for the most part people jostled each other for a good view from the temple steps or from the sidelines.

Likewise, the combatants were equipped in similarly makeshift fashion. Some fought dressed in their underwear and armed just with a spear or a sword. This produced short, fatal fights. Before long the families staging the munera began looking for ways to make the gladiatorial fights last longer and be more entertaining. At the games organized for Flaminius the fighters seem to have used a version of standard Roman army equipment. Provided with shields, mail jackets and helmets, the fighters had the chance to put up some form of defence against attack, making the fights more of a contest of skill than they had been.

Soon after this it became the custom to strip the gladiators of body armour, leaving them with just shield and helmet for defence. A sword thrust to the body was therefore more likely to prove fatal. The prime purpose of these games was still to sacrifice slaves to honour the dead, so wounds needed to end in death rather than mere injury.

It was at this period that the word 'gladiator' was developed. Fighters were no longer equipped with an assortment of weapons such as spears or lances, but were mostly confined to the basic sword of the Roman army infantry. This was a heavy, short sword with a fairly broad blade and excessively sharp point. Its main use was for stabbing, with its tip able to slip around shields or into chinks in armour. The weapon had been borrowed from warriors in Spain and was known as the *gladius hispanensis*. A man who used such a weapon was a 'gladiator'.

Other gladiatorial equipment of this time was also similar to that found in the army. The shield most often used by these unfortunate men was large and rectangular or oval. It could measure over four feet from top to bottom and curved round at the sides to deflect incoming blows. The helmet tended to be made of bronze and had a round crown, long neck guard and large cheek pieces.

In the years after 150 BC a distinct change came over the gladiatorial games. No longer was their prime purpose to kill men to honour the noble dead. Instead the real purpose was to honour the living and gain prestige and advancement for those staging the games. The reason behind the changing emphasis was the enormous popularity of the gladiatorial combats. Watching real fights with sharp weapons between real men, albeit slaves, was an exciting and thrilling activity. If a munus included gladiators the citizens of Rome would attend in their thousands. In 165 BC the playwright Publius Terentius Afer, generally known today as Terence, put on his finest play, *The Mother in Law*. Halfway through a packed performance a rumour ran round that a gladiatorial show due for later that day was about to start early. The theatre emptied, leaving Terence and his actors with no audience at all.

At first this great popularity was accepted by the patrician families who staged gladiatorial munera as a tribute to the dead man being honoured. The more people who came to the show, the better for the honour of the departed spirit and for the family staging it. Before long, however, aspiring politicians began using the games as a means of boosting their careers. Where previously the emphasis had been on the dead man owed the munus, the centre of attention now shifted to be on the man staging the games. And while the earlier games had been primarily to kill men, they now had as their primary object the entertainment of the crowd of voting citizens who attended.

One of the first moves to be made was to stage the munera not in the cattle market but in the Roman Forum. This was the largest open space in Rome, located in the very centre of the city. There was enough space in the Forum for wooden stands to be erected around the fighting area, something not possible in the smaller Forum Boarium. These seats meant the audience could both sit comfortably and get a clear view of the action. These stands were taken down immediately after the munera so that the Forum could revert to its usual function of being a centre for business and religion. The costs of staging a munus were rising, but so was the political benefit to be gained.

In 53 BC a young patrician named Gaius Scribonius Curio, hoping for a political career, was given the opportunity to win favour with the voters by staging a munus for his father, a former consul and famous orator who had been occupying the post of chief priest of Rome when he died. Unfortunately for young Curio his father had not left much in the way of money for the munus. Undaunted, Curio decided to go for quality rather than quantity in staging his spectacle to impress the Romans.

Curio announced that the munus for his father would consist of theatre shows in the morning and gladiators in the afternoon. He then set his carpenters to work building the necessary wooden stands for the spectators, but Curio kept the works hidden behind large hoardings.

When the day for the munus came, the crowds of citizens filed in to see two wooden theatres. The seats were raised up in great banks and arranged in semi-circles placed back to back. Curio was staging one play in one theatre and another play in the other theatre. The acoustics and stage machinery were arranged so that the one did not intrude on the other. It was most impressive.

But Curio's greatest trick was yet to come. When the plays ended, the audience was asked to remain in their seats. Then the seats began to shiver, shake and to move. Curio had mounted the entire wooden seating tiers on rollers, and these were now being pushed by an army of slaves. As the banked seats moved they swivelled around a pivot so that the back-to-back arrangement was reversed and the seats now faced each other across a circular central arena. In rode Curio to the cheers of the masses. The lack of numbers in the gladiatorial combats which then followed was forgotten by the crowd who were overwhelmed by the novelty of the proceedings.

Curio was promptly elected to be Tribune, going on to become governor of Sicily and a high ranking general. Such were the rewards for a man who could put on a successful munus.

While changes to the staging of the games were being made, so too were alterations to the games themselves. Politicians were keen to put on more memorable and more popular shows. By 100 BC merely setting men to fight each other was no longer enough. Novelty was needed. The answer was not long in coming.

East of the Appenine Mountains from Rome lived a people known as the Samnites. These people had fought several wars against Rome between 343 BC and 290 BC, after which their country became a tributary state. In 90 BC the Samnites rebelled but were defeated fairly quickly by an army led by Lucius Cornelius Sulla. By chance Sulla was a descendant of Publius Cornelius Rufinus who had defeated the Samnites in 290 BC. Eager to be elected Consul, Sulla naturally decided to stage a munus.

To add novelty and excitement to his games, Sulla brought a number of Samnite prisoners to fight in the arena. To add even more reality to the bloody spectacle these men were equipped with the same arms and armour they had used in the recent war. The Samnites had long been famous for the quality of their armaments, so the mob were eager to see Samnites fight with their native weapons.

The Samnites in the arena appeared equipped with a large rectangular shield, not too different from that used by the Romans, and with metal greaves to protect the shins below the shield. The weapon carried by them was a medium-length straight sword with a single cutting edge. It was the helmet which made the Samnite such an outstanding sight. The rounded metal crown was topped by an extravagant upright ridge which itself sprouted a stiff crest of dyed horse hair. Around the edge of the helmet was a wide metal brim. Rising from the junction between brim and helmet was a pair of flamboyant feathers, usually from pheasants or even peacocks.

The Samnites were a huge success with the crowd. Sulla was elected Consul and given command of the army sent to defeat King Mithradates of Pontus. He came back to be elected Dictator, an unusual and temporary post created only in times of crisis, and to rule Rome until he retired to his country estate in 79 BC.

The success of the Samnites in gaining favour with the crowd led other politicians to bring in foreign fighters. First to appear, in about 80 BC, were some from the country of Thrace, which was roughly the region of modern Bulgaria. The Thracians were a notoriously wild and warlike people who herded sheep and cattle and launched regular raids into the Roman province of Macedonia to their south. Their warlike nature was no doubt easily believed in by the Romans as the son of Mars, Roman god of war, was named Thrax.

A few Thracian prisoners of war were brought to Rome to fight in the arena as a result of border wars. These men were armed in a new and exciting fashion. They had smaller shields and wore more extensive leg armour together with a round helmet topped by an animal-shaped ornament. The main weapon they carried was a stout, sharply curved sword rather like a sickle, though with the cutting edge on the outside of the curve.

Not long afterwards, Gauls began to appear in the arena. These men came from the area which is now southern France, brought into conflict with Rome because the Romans held the Greek colonies around Marseilles and the mouth of the Rhone. Again these unfortunates were undoubtedly prisoners of war set to fight with their native arms and armour. They would have worn simple helmets, often conical in shape, but little else in the way of armour. Their main weapon was a long, heavy sword used for slashing at the enemy rather than for thrusting. Most Gauls carried large upright shields made of wood covered with leather, often painted with bright abstract patterns.

These innovations were enormously popular, so much so that when the original Samnites, Thracians and Gauls died or were retired their arms and armour were passed on to new gladiators. Although still called by the original national names, these men were not native to the lands whose armour they carried. The terms had come to mean merely a type of gladiator, rather than to describe the nationality of the man fighting.

As time passed more and more types of gladiator were introduced to the arena. Some types failed to become popular and were quickly dropped. Others gained favour with the mob and remained regular features of the games for centuries.

As the motive of the games increasingly shifted towards impressing the mob, the actual business of killing became secondary. Death remained a vital element of the events in the arena, but it was no longer enough to send a few slaves to hack clumsily at each other until one of them died. The crowd now expected displays of swordsmanship and well-developed fighting skills. For a while the prisoners of war, themselves trained warriors, supplied the necessary level of skill. But a steady supply of such men relied on Roman victory in warfare, and that could not be guaranteed. Patricians eager to put on a spectacular munus could not rely on the chancy business of there being a glut of prisoners available.

This led to the key development in the history of the gladiators. By about 75 BC the men fighting in the arena were no longer cheap, second rate slaves sent to die. They were highly trained, skilled fighting men at the peak of physical fitness. Only these men could put on the sort of show that would win favour with the crowd. Such men were, however, hugely expensive to train, equip and maintain. Very often they were simply too expensive to kill.

Thus the custom of the *missus* appeared. A gladiator who was clearly losing a fight could throw down his shield and raise his left arm in token of surrender. His life was then at the mercy of the organizer of the games. If the organizer felt the man had fought well and bravely he would be given the missus, meaning he could leave the arena alive. If the man had not fought well, the missus would be refused and the man killed. Of course, even the most skilled man might fall victim to a fatal sword thrust in combat at any time.

Once it became fairly common for gladiators to survive losing a fight, the possibility arose of gladiators spending years fighting time and again in the arena. Although most gladiators remained slaves, they could look forward to a career not noticeably more dangerous than that of a soldier. Big, tough men who trained hard and gained skill with weaponry might survive for years, eventually becoming the trainers of the next generation.

This dramatic improvement in the life expectancy of a gladiator in turn led to the development of the *familia gladiatorae*, the troupe of gladiators. No single patrician family could afford to keep, train and feed a host of professional gladiators against the occasional time the family would be called upon to stage a munus. Instead, gladiatorial schools were organized led by a man known as a *lanista*. The lanista would rent out his troupe of men to the person staging the munus. This system was to become increasingly complex as time passed.

By the middle of the first century BC, the fully developed system of gladiatorial combat and organization which was to survive to the fall of Rome had evolved. The original purpose of sacrificing humans at a funeral had been long forgotten, though the munera were still ostensibly staged to honour a famous man who had died. Gone too were the clumsy combats of household slaves pushed untrained into the arena. The gladiators were now professionals. Their trade was violent and deadly, but disease and deprivation made life expectancy in Rome fairly short anyway.

The strange and violent institution of the games had been established. Now Rome was set to take the spectacle to new heights of extravagance and violence.

Rebel gladiator leader Spartacus, pictured here in Eastern attire. The bravery and fighting skills of the rebel gladiators were never in doubt, but their lack of discipline would eventually prove fatal. They were defeated at the River Silarus by a Roman army led by Marcus Crassus. Crassus had 6,000 captured rebels crucified along the road from Capua, where the revolt had begun, to Rome, as a warning to others.

II
SPARTACUS

IN 73 BC the gladiatorial system was developing rapidly. The earlier regime under which the gladiators were untrained slaves pushed into mortal combat was over. Nor was it any longer obligatory for the defeated fighter to be put to death so that his blood could satisfy the honour of a departed hero. On the other hand the sophisticated and formalized programmes of combat and spectacle were not yet developed.

An emerging feature of the system at this time was the gladiatorial school where slaves were trained to fight using specialized gladiator weapons. The lives of such men would be short and hard. A few might survive long enough to become trainers of gladiators, or suffer crippling wounds that would send them to work in the kitchens, but these would be a minority. The rest had only death to look forward to.

Among the most poorly treated were the captured prisoners of war condemned to fight in the arena for the benefit of the Roman people. These men were not only slaves, but also enemies of Rome and could expect little mercy. One such man was a Thracian named Spartacus. According to one account he had spent some years as a mercenary in the Roman army. He had certainly gained some experience of military command before being captured and sent to a gladiatorial training school at Capua in Campania.

Later accounts alleged that one night soon after his capture a snake coiled itself around Spartacus' head while he lay sleeping. This, his wife foretold, meant that he would one day have great power, but that it would bring him misfortune and disaster.

One day in the spring of 73 BC, Spartacus organized a break out from the gladiatorial school at Capua. He was assisted by a Gaul named Crixus. The school held about 200 gladiators at the time. The plan was secretly to get hold of some kitchen knives or spits to use as weapons, then overpower the guards and make a break for freedom. Lentulus Batiates, who owned the school, heard a rumour of the coming break out and segregated the gladiators. As a result only seventy-eight gladiators, plus a few wives and domestic slaves managed to get out.

As the escapees raced through the streets of Capua they found a cart loaded with gladiatorial weapons and equipment, which they seized. They fought their way past the city guards at the gate and headed into the open country. Once out of the city, Spartacus and Crixus led the band towards the huge volcano of Vesuvius, then dormant and believed to be extinct.

Knowing that pursuit was inevitable, the gladiators holed up at the summit of the volcano where only one narrow path gave access to the crater. The local Roman commander, Claudius Glaber was jubilant. He marched his force up to the narrow entrance to the path and blockaded it. Glaber reasoned that hunger and thirst would soon persuade the renegades to surrender.

Glaber was, however, wrong. He had marched into a trap. Spartacus and his men had stripped the crater of the large numbers of wild vines that grew there and twisted them into rope ladders. Using these, the gladiators had let themselves down the sheer cliffs which had seemed to hem them in. Marching swiftly around the mountain the gladiators fell upon the rear of Glaber, taking his force entirely by surprise. The Romans could not use their superior numbers in the confined space of the narrow path and those that could not flee were cut down.

Rome now sent a praetor, a senior government official, named Publius Varinius with several thousand troops to capture Spartacus and his renegades. By the time Varinius arrived in Campania, however, Spartacus had gathered together several thousand runaway slaves who had been only too eager to escape from the harsh conditions on the slave estates which covered much of the farming land in southern Italy.

Varinius found himself unexpectedly outnumbered and was defeated.

When news of this victory for Spartacus spread, the cities of Campania locked their gates and sent appeals to Rome for help. The slaves, however, left their farms and workshops in their thousands to flock to join the runaways. It was now autumn, so Spartacus led his mixed force of men, women and children south to Thurii, now Terranova.

There Spartacus extorted food and supplies from nearby cities under threat of unleashing his forces to destroy them. Several bands of the renegades roamed the countryside in search of loot and raping and murdering. Spartacus did his best to stop them but did not have the means of imposing strict discipline. Meanwhile the winter was spent in training the more amenable able-bodied men in rudimentary battle tactics and weapons drill.

The following spring, Spartacus and Crixus led their force north. They intended to march quickly, crossing the Alps in mid summer and then dispersing back to their homelands. As they marched, the force divided in two so that it could live off the land as it passed through. The rebel leaders needed to be careful of supplies, for their mass of followers by this date was huge. One ancient writer guesses Spartacus had 70,000 people with him, another puts the figure at 120,000. It is, in fact, impossible to know how large the force was, but it was clearly numerous and aggressive.

The Romans sent out four legions led by the Consuls Lucius Gellius and Lentulus Clodianus to defeat the slave army. The Consuls caught Crixus near Mount Garganus and utterly defeated his force, killing him in the battle. Spartacus and his men arrived before the Romans could reform and defeated both Consuls in turn. Gathering 300 prisoners, Spartacus forced them to fight as gladiators, killing their comrades to save their own lives. Clearly the Thracian had a sense of irony.

Moving north again, Spartacus and his men defeated the Roman governor of northern Italy outside Modena. The road to the Alpine passes was open. At this point Spartacus changed his mind, or had it changed for him by his followers. Instead of continuing north over the Alps, the army of renegade slaves turned back south. Some of them wanted to attack Rome itself, but Spartacus was wary of such an enterprise. Instead he led his forces against the now unprotected cities of Campania and

Lucania. Some cities fell and were pillaged, others cowered behind their walls and hoped starvation would cause Spartacus to move on.

The Romans, meanwhile, had elected the stupendously rich financier Marcus Licinius Crassus to be praetor, raised a fresh army and sent him at its head to defeat Spartacus. Crassus had a particular interest in defeating the rebels for he used large numbers of slaves to farm his estates. Crassus had served with the dictator Sulla in his youth and retained enough military skill to realize it was better to harry the army of runaways rather than risk an open battle. Day after day, week after week, Crassus dogged Spartacus as the slaves headed south. Crassus ambushed and cut down any men Spartacus sent out to gather food or supplies.

By the late summer of 71 BC Spartacus and his men were confined to the toe of Italy. Crassus set his soldiers to digging a deep ditch backed by a timber and earth wall from sea to sea. He was determined to pen the rebels in and starve them into surrender.

In desperation, Spartacus hired a fleet of pirates to transport his forces to Sicily. He hoped not only to escape Crassus, but also to raise the slaves of Sicily in revolt. This would not only have increased the size of his rapidly shrinking army, but would have given him a reasonably secure base of operations. Unfortunately the pirates took the money, but then sailed off.

Next Spartacus took those of his followers who were fit and active and broke through the siege lines of Crassus. It is unclear where Spartacus was trying to lead his men, perhaps he was just hoping to get away from Crassus or reach some supposed supplies of food. Wherever he was going, Spartacus was not moving fast enough. The Roman scouts kept a careful watch on the slave army.

Turning in his tracks, Spartacus drove off the pursuing scouts in a brief skirmish. This small victory convinced the runaway slaves that they could defeat the main Roman force. They were, in any case, tired of running. Short of supplies and with his men demanding action, Spartacus decided to attack. Having avoided battle before, Crassus now welcomed the fight as he believed he had sufficiently weakened his enemy.

The battle was fought on the banks of the River Silarus. From the very first the Romans got the better of the slaves. In a final charge,

Spartacus tried to reach Crassus, but was cut down in the attempt. With their leader dead, the army of slaves and gladiators collapsed. Some fled, some surrendered, some killed themselves.

As a slave owner, Crassus was determined to use the defeated rebels as a terrible lesson to other slaves. He selected 6,000 at random and had them crucified on a line of crosses that ran the entire length of the road from Capua, where the rebellion had begun, to the gates of Rome. The men took days to die in agony, and their bodies were left to rot to pieces. The grim road signs served to tell anyone who passed that way what fate awaited those gladiators or slaves who thought to escape the fate allotted to them by Roman law.

Crassus, of course, hoped to benefit politically from his success. He had spent many months in the field fighting a gruelling campaign against a wily adversary who had defeated several other Roman generals. He was, however, to be disappointed. Even as Crassus was fighting his battle on the banks of the Silarus, Rome's most famous general Gnaeus Pompeius, known as Pompey, was marching south to help defeat the rebels. Pompey met a band of about 5,000 escaped slaves and wiped them out. He then got back to Rome before Crassus and managed to take the credit for crushing the rebellion.

Despite his terrible cruelty to the defeated rebels, Crassus himself did not treat his own slaves badly. He gave them good food and rarely inflicted severe punishments, but not all were like him

Trying to asses the impact of the revolt led by Spartacus on the status of slaves is difficult. Those who had joined Spartacus had come mostly from the extensive agricultural estates where large gangs of slaves worked in dreadful conditions. The majority of slaves, living in households or working in small-scale workshops, had remained largely unaffected. As it is the latter class which feature most often in surviving written records, information about estate slaves is hard to come by. We do know, however, that large estates continued to be farmed by slave labour.

The impact of the uprising on gladiators was more immediate and better recorded. The armed guards stationed at gladiatorial barracks and schools were increased dramatically. The weapons, previously stored at the barracks, were removed for storage in stronghouses elsewhere.

Discipline was made harsher and punishments for insubordination were more severe. In the immediate aftermath of the revolt, life for a gladiator became much harder than it had been.

Conversely, some leading politicians learned a very different lesson from the troubles. They saw how effective the gladiators had been in battle. Soon many leading patricians were acquiring and running gladiatorial schools. These gladiators did not do much in the way of actual fighting, and they were trained in some very unusual skills. They were taught how to move through city streets at night without attracting attention. They were taught how to administer poison and slit throats. They learnt how to force a path through an angry mob, how to disarm attackers and how to break limbs.

These slaves were big, tough men who were housed in gladiatorial barracks and lived by the gladiatorial code, but they were not gladiators as most people then or now understand the word. They were the private strong arm gangs of unscrupulous politicians. Romans were forbidden to recruit and train private armies, but in their gangs of gladiators the ruthless men of power had the next best thing.

In 63 BC the reign of terror these gladiators were creating came to a crisis point. That year the cunning, dissolute young aristocrat Lucius Sergius Catalina, known as Catiline, was defeated in the election for Consul by the orator Marcus Tullius Cicero, though Catiline's friend Gaius Antoninus was elected as the second consul. Catiline and Antoninus had planned to use their positions as Consuls to instigate a wide ranging revolution in society that would, among other things, have cancelled debt for the poor, stripped the rich of their wealth and led to the executions of many people disliked by Catiline and Antoninus.

The Catiline plan had to take place in 63 BC as the great general Pompey was due back in Rome the following year and would have had the authority and force to stamp it out. The only way the two friends could forward their aims was to murder Cicero and force a fresh election. Catiline turned to his 'gladiators' to accomplish the death of his rival. As the autumn approached street fights and riots were orchestrated until Rome was in turmoil. Catiline planned to mass his gladiators around the Senate house for the meeting on 7 November. He would then start a riot in the course of which Cicero and his supporters would be murdered.

Cicero, however, was informed of the plot in time to organize an armed guard of soldiers for the crucial Senate meeting. Catiline and his men fled, to be hunted down and killed by his one time ally Gaius Antoninus for whom cold-blooded murder of half the senate had been a step too far.

Rather surprisingly the defeat of Catiline did nothing to halt the use of 'gladiators' for street violence and political thuggery. Riots and bloodshed were to grow steadily worse as normal concepts of democracy broke down. Within a few years of the Catiline conspiracy civil law in Rome had become defied to such an extent that leading politicians no longer needed to pretend their private armies were gladiators. Those gladiators whose skills lay in civil strife were now openly kept as armed slaves. The others reverted to their original role as entertainers.

Gladiators disappeared from the open political arena and returned to the bloodstained sands from which they had come. This was a time when the gladiators were to be used in numbers never before seen.

Perhaps better known today as a philosopher, the emperor Marcus Aurelius was one of the few Roman rulers who did not relish the gladiatorial games. He rarely attended the slaughters in the arena and never staged special games to delight the mob.

III
˒ THE GREAT GAMES ˒

THE BLOODY GAMES in the arena had, by 100 BC, become a primary tool in the campaign of any ambitious politician. Winning votes meant pleasing the Roman mob and there was no better way to do this than to entertain them. Many of the voting public were poor to the point of destitution and looked on the games as the only luxury available to them.

Of all the games, the gladiatorial contests were the most use to a politician. Not only were they hugely popular but they were outside the scope of the state spectacles. Nearly every other form of popular mass entertainment was either staged by the state or closely controlled by it. Only the violent combats, descended as they were from private funeral rites, were entirely under the control of the person who staged them.

A man wishing to win the votes of the crowd needed only the flimsiest of excuses to stage a *munus*, as these obligatory shows to honour the dead were known. Although in theory they could be staged only as part of a funeral, they were often held months or even years after the death of the person supposedly being honoured. The timing of elections in which the heirs putting on the shows were candidates was the key determining factor.

In 79 BC the victorious general Gnaeus Pompeius returned from Africa having defeated a rebellion with remarkable speed and efficiency. On his return to Rome, Pompey was heaped with praise by the dictator Sulla, who gave him the surname ' Magnus, meaning 'The Great'. In celebration of his victory, Pompey announced that he was to put on a series of games.

At first Sulla tried to stop Pompey, fearing that the increasingly popular general, although a firm supporter of his, might gain too much favour from the mob and become a rival. Sulla invoked an old law stating that a Roman who did not belong to the Patrician class, as Pompey did not, could not stage games unless he had first held a senior government post. Pompey was thirty-five years old at the time and had spent his career in the army, not in government. Pompey had a clear sense of the importance of the mob of Roman citizens and appealed to them directly, over the heads of the magistrates and the law. Sulla gave way with grace, though he later cut Pompey from his will, and the great games of Pompey went ahead.

Pompey announced that his games were to be so lavish that they could not be held in the Forum with the crowd watching from temporary wooden stands. Instead, Pompey commandeered the Circus Maximus. This vast stadium was built for chariot racing and could seat over 100,000 people at this date. Although the seating was ready made, Pompey put men to work, this time erecting iron gratings and other barriers between the crowd and the floor of the race track. Gladiators were so heavily guarded that there was little likelihood that they would attack the crowd or seek to escape, so the citizens wondered what the barriers were for. Pompey had a surprise.

During his campaign in North Africa, Pompey had been forced to face war elephants. These animals were highly trained and would attack cavalrymen or infantry. They could be ordered to trample any living creature which got in their path, or to use their trunks to hurl victims high into the air, to crash to their deaths. Even the elephants' tusks were brought into play to spear unfortunate victims or to crush them against the ground. Over a century earlier, Hannibal had brought a handful of elephants to Italy over the Alps, but it was in North Africa that the Romans had had to face war elephants in any great numbers.

Pompey had brought twenty of these formidable animals to Rome to take part in his spectacular games. To face these ferocious beasts, Pompey had two groups of men. The first were a band of unfortunates who were to be little more than victims – they were probably condemned criminals. These men were given weapons and armour before being sent into the Circus Maximus but, without any sort of training, were no match for the war elephants. They were swiftly killed.

The second group Pompey had to hand were highly skilled hunters from the nomadic Getuli tribe of North Africa. These men had been recruited by King Bocchus of Mauretania, a country on the northwestern edge of the Sahara. The Getuli were famed in North Africa for their ability to kill or capture elephants, but this was unknown in Rome. To the tens of thousands of Romans watching Pompey's games the foreigners appeared to be just another group of men being sent to the slaughter.

As the elephants roamed the bloodstained arena, the Getuli moved in on one individual. As the elephant rushed forwards, the Getuli pretended to flee, but a single man stood his ground. The Romans fully expected him to be reduced to a mangled pulp in seconds. Instead, the hunter threw his heavy hunting spear so that it struck the elephant just below the eye, smashing through the skull bones, which were thin at that spot, and penetrating the brain. The elephant fell dead on the spot. The crowd cheered.

Next the Getuli surrounded a lone elephant and began running around it. As the bewildered animal tried to concentrate on the swiftly moving men, the Getuli hurled spears at its feet, literally nailing it to the arena floor so that it could not move. A hunter then closed in and slit the elephants throat. The crowd cheered again.

The Getuli tried the same trick on the next elephant, but this one tore its feet free, and made a grab for the hunters. It got hold of a shield, which it tore from the hunter's arm and threw aside. Now the Getuli had to run in fear. The crowd loved it and roared with laughter.

Pompey, prominently seated in the stands, must have beamed. His games were proving a huge success and popularity was bound to follow.

Then things went wrong.

After a few more elephants had been killed, the survivors gathered into a herd at the centre of the Circus Maximus. The Getuli hunters tried to separate individuals out from the herd, but the elephants were having none of it. As one, they suddenly charged forwards, straight towards the crowds of Romans citizens. The charging beasts crashed into the iron grilles, which buckled and partly collapsed. Quickly the Getuli moved in to hamstring and cut down the leading elephants.

The few surviving beasts retreated to the centre of the Circus Maximus. There they put on a remarkable display, recorded by an ancient writer. 'The beasts withdrew from the fight covered with wounds. They walked about with their trunks raised towards heaven, weeping so bitterly as to give rise to the report that they did not do so by mere chance but were crying out against the oaths in which they had trusted when they crossed over from Africa and calling on the gods to avenge them. It was recalled that they had refused to board the ships before they received a pledge from their handlers that they would not be harmed at all in Rome.'

The crowd, frightened by the elephants' charge and by the risk of sudden death if the elephants had got through the barriers, began to curse Pompey. They blamed him for not taking proper precautions, and some demanded that the surviving elephants should be allowed to live and be sent back to Africa.

Somewhat chastened, Pompey the Great went back to the army and postponed his political ambitions for another eight years. His idea of staging animal hunts was, however, a daring one. It was to be copied by other politicians eager to court publicity and fame, though they took great care to ensure the safety of the crowd.

One of these ambitious men was Gaius Julius Caesar. Born to an impoverished branch of the hugely respected and aristocratic Julian clan, Caesar was an ambitious young man. When his father died in 85 BC, Caesar held only a modest funeral and refused to stage a *munus*. Twenty years later Caesar was elected as one of the four Aediles, a fairly junior position which put him in charge of the weights and measures used in the markets, the fire brigade and public health. The Aediles were also responsible for ensuring certain religious festivals were held correctly. Caesar now announced that the time had come for his father's munus.

Caesar knew that he needed to put on a truly outstanding show for the citizens of Rome if his political ambitions were to come to anything in a city dominated by richer and more prestigious men, such as Pompey the Great. Pompey was now back in politics and was hugely popular. Caesar turned to Marcus Licinius Crassus. It had been Crassus who had defeated the slave revolt of Spartacus, but had seen Pompey take the credit. Crassus was therefore willing to invest some of his stupendous wealth in furthering the career of a rival to Pompey.

Armed with the money of Crassus, Caesar began preparing for the munus to honour his father. For months, Caesar and his agents scoured Italy for gladiators. Entire schools were bought up and thousands of fighting men were hired for the games. Pompey's supporters were alarmed. They not only feared the popularity Caesar would gain from such games, but also were genuinely alarmed that having so many armed men in Rome at one time would be a serious threat to law and order. They hurriedly passed a law banning gladiatorial shows in which more than 320 pairs of fighters took part.

Caesar was undaunted. He made certain everyone in Rome knew that it was Pompey's supporters who had robbed them of the most spectacular games of all time. Then he held his games with 320 pairs of gladiators. Each man was dressed in a suit of armour specially made from solid silver.

Caesar's munus for his father were a huge success, as much for the blame Caesar heaped on his political opponents as for the popularity he gained for himself. The hugely expensive silver armour was then rented out to other patricians wanting to put on a show. When its novelty value had worn off, the armour was melted down and sold as bullion.

With his political future assured by such a successful gladiatorial show, Caesar embarked on a career which proved to be a tortured affair. First he was opposed to Pompey, then allied to him, then engaged in a civil war against him which cost thousands of Roman lives. Finally, in 46 BC, Caesar returned to Rome to take up the position of Dictator, as had Sulla before him in similar conditions of civil unrest. Unlike Sulla, however, Caesar had himself appointed Dictator for life. He knew the Romans would not care for such a violation of their much treasured republican system, so he laid on a series of games to win popularity for himself and his new powers.

Caesar spared nothing in the way of expense or trouble for the great games of 46 BC. He arranged for theatre shows and chariot racing to take place day after day. He brought dancers from every corner of the Roman Empire, and beyond, to show off their national costumes and dances to the crowd. Trick riders and jugglers were hired in large numbers. He brought foreign royalty to Rome to flatter the crowd by making protestations of friendship and support for Rome. He flooded some low-lying ground near the city and staged fake naval fights between real warships. He brought strange and exotic animals to Rome for display to the crowds. The most popular of these was the giraffe. No such animal had ever been seen before and its ungainly movements brought roars of laughter from the crowd.

But most important were the gladiatorial games. Again, Caesar made sure they were the finest ever.

Caesar's first stunt was to stage a battle unique in Roman history. He put two senators into the arena to fight to the death. Furius Leptinus and Quintus Calpenus were both senior members of patrician families of great honour and pride, but they had chosen to support Pompey and now faced death. Caesar offered them the chance to live if they fought in the arena. For the vast crowds of plebeian citizens the sight of two such proud and haughty men spilling blood for the entertainment of the mob was irresistible. Snobbery was rife among Rome's elite and here it was turned on its head. Caesar cleverly flattered his voting public with the blood of his enemies.

The main gladiatorial fights were, as usual, staged in a temporary stadium in the Roman Forum. Caesar's stadium improved on earlier models by having the fights take place on a raised platform, underneath which were located hidden tunnels, trap doors and lifts. Fights were interrupted by such novelties as the sudden release of a lion from a lift or the emergence of new gladiators.

The final spectacle of the great games of 46 BC took place, as did that of Pompey's games thirty years earlier, in the Circus Maximus. Again the event involved war elephants. Caesar, however, had arranged for two armies to camp out in the chariot stadium, each force consisting of 500 infantry, thirty cavalry and twenty war elephants. The ensuing battle between the slave armies lasted hours and ended only with the complete annihilation of one side.

The stupendous games had cost Caesar a vast fortune, but they had bought him absolute power in Rome. Or so he thought. In fact a small group of senior senators deeply resented the fact that he had taken dictatorial powers not just for a few years to sort out the chaos the Republic had fallen into, but for life. Fewer than two years after Caesar staged his great games, he was murdered. Ironically he was stabbed to death when standing at the base of a statue of his old rival, Pompey.

After Caesar's death a new civil war broke out. The chaos was not ended until Caesar's nephew, Gaius Octavian Caesar, defeated his rivals and took supreme power. The victory of Octavian, known to history as Augustus, had a profound effect on the gladiatorial games. Augustus, and all later emperors, forbade anyone to put on *munera* or spectacles without their permission. The continual rivalry between ambitious politicians to put on bigger and better games that had dominated the previous century came to an end.

Instead, the prime purpose of the games came to be the establishment and maintenance of the popularity of the Emperor. Magnificent and spectacular as the gladiatorial and other games might have been under the Empire, there was no longer a desperate imperative to find new and novel ways to titillate the crowds. Instead the gladiatorial games became institutionalized. With a steady demand for an increasingly standardized form of display and combat, the gladiator industry could become organized and regularized as never before.

While there remained a clear need for the Emperors to put on lavish shows to please the vast crowd of voters that made up the Roman mob, there was no longer any competition. No emperor had to worry about what sort of a show a rival politician would be staging in a few months time. There were no rival politicians. As a result innovation and new ideas gradually became less important than sheer spectacle and magnificence.

Augustus led the way. In 29 BC an otherwise rather obscure general named Titus Statilius Taurus was granted permission by Augustus to hold a gladiatorial munus. Permission was granted in thanks for a successful campaign Taurus had commanded in North Africa, but the permission came with conditions. Taurus had to spend money building a permanent arena for gladiatorial shows to replace the temporary wooden stands erected in the Forum. The general accordingly built a structure with lower stories of stone and upper stories of wood in the Campus Martius. This was a stretch of flat ground north of the city used for military training and parades.

Taurus' building was the first permanent home for the gladiatorial contests. Typically, Augustus had his own name carved over the entrance to ensure everyone knew that the structure was erected at his insistence.

Augustus also put on his own gladiatorial games. Details of these are rather sketchy, but he later recorded for posterity 'Three times I held a gladiatorial spectacle in my own name and five times in the names of my sons or grandsons. In these games some 10,000 men took part. I have provided spectacles of hunting wild beasts twenty-six times in my own name or that of my sons and grandsons, in the Circus or the Forum or the Amphitheatre, in which 3,500 beasts have been killed.' Such entertainments were spectacles indeed, but Augustus added nothing new. Compared to Sulla and his Samnites, Pompey and his elephants or Caesar and his mock naval fight, Augustus brought nothing novel to the games he promoted.

Tiberius, the emperor after Augustus, did even less. He cut back on the money spent on gladiatorial spectacles, so secure was he in power. His great nephew, Caligula, by contrast loved the games and quickly raced through the state treasury by staging larger and more impressive displays than had been customary before. By the time of Caligula the various types of gladiatorial fighter were becoming well defined. The young emperor chose to train with the weapons and in the skills of a Thracian gladiator. This was not considered eccentric, by then all young noblemen undertook military training of one sort or another.

Caligula's infatuation with the Thracians turned more dangerous, however, when he began favouring them in the arena. If a Thracian lost a fight he was far more likely to gain a *missus*, that is to say to be allowed to live, than any other type of fighter. Things reached a head when a popular gladiator named Columbus defeated a Thracian, but was wounded in the process. Caligula had the victor poisoned in a fit of spite. This act of wanton unfairness, which robbed Rome of one of its finest gladiators, lost Caligula the popularity with the crowd that he had been courting so carefully. Sensing their chance, a group of senators and army officers opposed to Caligula's increasingly bizarre and arbitrary rule hatched a plot and murdered the emperor.

Clearly losing favour with the mob at the games could be dangerous. Later emperors rarely forgot the example of Caligula. His uncle and successor Claudius put on some impressive shows, including a mock naval fight on Lake Fucino. Nero was less fond of gladiatorial combat, but lavished theatrical shows and chariot racing on the Romans. He went so far as to appear on stage himself, being a not untalented poet and singer.

For the next four centuries Rome would see a unique and gory industry which employed tens of thousands and led to the brutal deaths of thousands. The gladiatorial games as they are known to history were born.

Ave Caesar, morituri te salutant! ('Hail Caesar, we who are about to die salute you!')
A group of gladiators gives the traditional salute to the Emperor in the Circus
Maximus.

IV

، TRAINING THE ،
GLADIATORS

T HE WAYS IN WHICH GLADIATORS were recruited, trained and maintained was, for the Romans, a distinctly dishonourable business. Few citizens of any consequence got involved except as a mask for hiring a gang of street toughs, and so accounts of these matters emerge only slowly into the written record.

We know that in the earliest days of the gladiatorial *munera*, the gladiators were largely recruited from amongst the personal slaves of the man whose funeral rites were being celebrated. Those slaves who would previously have been earmarked for sacrifice were put to fighting each other to the death instead. Often the dying man would specify in his will which slaves were to be used as gladiators and how much money his heirs should spend on entertaining the crowd of citizens which was bound to turn up to watch. One patrician stipulated that the gladiators who fought and died at his *munus* should be the teenage slaves he had bought to be his homosexual lovers. The youth of the proposed victims and the manifest unfairness of the man's will led the magistrates to overturn it. Older men were chosen to fight instead.

During Rome's long wars of expansion through the Republic and early Imperial periods there was a ready supply of prisoners of war. These were trained soldiers who could be pushed into the arena with little need for preparation. Nor were they particularly expensive, so those who died meant little in the way of financial loss to those staging the games. The survivors could be sold to citizens wanting gladiators or put to work on farms and in workshops.

By the middle of the first century AD, however, the situation had changed markedly. The demand for gladiators and arena games was as great as ever, but the ready supplies of prisoners of war were no longer available. To remedy this difficulty an entire business grew up to recruit, train and maintain the gladiators. The key figure in the gladiator industry was the *lanista*.

The man known as the lanista was the owner and business manager of a troupe of gladiators, or *familia gladiatoria*. The gladiators were housed and trained at the school, the *ludi gladiatori*. The trade of a gladiator, and by extension that of the lanista, was considered rather disreputable in Roman society. A decent Roman citizen looked to earn a living with his brain or his skill, perhaps as a lawyer or a jeweller. Those who hired out their entire bodies for money were looked on as having sold themselves unworthily. Slaves fell into this category, as did prostitutes, actors and gladiators. It is not surprising, therefore, that most people who followed these despised trades actually were slaves. Even the lanista was as often as not a former slave desperate enough not to have the fine scruples of a citizen about what he did.

The lanista made his money by hiring out his troupe of gladiators to those who wished to stage a gladiatorial display, usually as part of a munus for a deceased relative. The scale of charges would be carefully worked out in advance and were subject to extensive negotiations between the lanista and his customer, known as the editor of the games. Not only were charges made for the number of gladiators appearing, but highly skilled fighters would cost a lot more than raw recruits. The types of gladiator used would also affect the price.

Most expensive of all would be the death of a gladiator. If a gladiator was killed during a munus, the lanista lost a valuable commodity which he would no longer be able to rent out. The lanista may have invested months or years of training, food and keep in the gladiator, all of which he would expect to be reimbursed for as well as the lost revenue of future rentals. For an editor to have gladiators fight to the death was an expensive business.

Gladiators who were killed in combat or died later of wounds were often charged to the lanista, but those gladiators who surrendered and asked for mercy were the responsibility of the editor. It was his decision whether a defeated man was granted the missus and allowed to live or was put to death in the arena. When a man appealed for mercy the watching crowd would make their feelings clearly known to the editor. They might have suggested mercy by holding up a clenched fist or they might have suggested death by shouting 'hoc habet', 'let him have it', or by making stabbing motions with their thumbs. An editor wishing to gain favour with crowd would have been inclined to grant their wishes, but killing too many gladiators might have cost a fortune. Mercy was often tempered with cold financial calculation.

It is worth mentioning the dispute over the signal used by Romans keen to decide the fate of a defeated gladiator. For many years it was thought that the thumbs up sign indicated the man was to live and the thumbs down sign that he was to die. It now seems more likely that hiding the thumb within the fist meant the sword should be sheathed, thus granting life, while a vigorous stabbing motion with the thumb indicated that the sword should be used. Whether that involved jabbing the thumb up or down appears to have been irrelevant.

In any case the final decision lay with the editor. There was little room for confusion in his signals. If he waved a handkerchief it meant the missus was granted. A derisory sweep of the bare hand, however, meant death.

As well as the cost of the gladiators, the lanista could charge for any extras, such as a suitably impressive parade chariot on which the editor could arrive to impress the crowd. The lanista usually had a whole host of other props available, including richly embroidered cloaks for the editor's family, special parade armour for the gladiators to use before entering combat, flags, banners and cushions to aid audience comfort.

The gladiators managed by the lanista were predominantly slaves. The lanista would buy these in the open slave markets which were found in most Roman towns. Naturally a lanista would look for big, strong men who promised to be good fighters. Such men might be captured prisoners of war, slaves surplus to a household or men from a slave farm who were no longer needed, or whose aggressive behaviour made them unwanted. Archeological digs have shown that the average height of a Roman male was about 5 feet 4 inches, but that soldiers averaged around

5 feet 6 inches. It is safe to assume that slaves purchased for use as gladiators would have been close to the height usual for soldiers.

Not all recruits to a gladiatorial school would be slaves. Some would be criminals who had been condemned to become gladiators, sometimes for a set number of years. But the most surprising recruits were free men, even citizens, who volunteered for this tough life. Some were driven to this extremity by debt. The lanista would pay for such a recruit and the money could be used to pay off creditors and allow the rest of the family to make a fresh start. Some young tearaways came for the excitement, thrill and glamour that they, as free gladiators, had the liberty to enjoy. As free men they would not be subjected to the same brutal discipline as the slaves, but if they were to survive they would need to undergo the same training regime.

By whatever means they were recruited, the new trainees would have to take an oath which bound them to loyalty to the lanista, and to accepting the whip, the branding iron and the sword as instruments of punishment. They would then be taken to the school itself. The gladiatorial training school at Pompeii has been excavated almost intact and can be used with written accounts to show what a typical ludi gladiatori would have looked like.

The main feature of any ludi was the training square around which were arranged the barracks, kitchens and other buildings. Some ludi had an oval enclosure the same size as a typical amphitheatre to allow gladiators who were about to appear in a munus to get accustomed to the size and shape of the arena. The barracks were a mixed affair. New recruits were placed in stark, windowless cells devoid of furniture other than piles of straw. The more experienced and more valuable veterans would have their own rooms, often comfortably furnished. Some even had a suite of rooms with accommodation for wives and children.

It was in the interests of the lanista to keep his gladiators in the peak of physical well being. The ludis therefore employed physicians and masseurs whose job was to ensure that the gladiators were fit and well. There were also cooks who were tasked with preparing nutritious and appetising meals for the gladiators, as well as preparing suitable food for the sick or injured. The mainstay of the diet was barley gruel, a food thought to promote good muscle tone and great strength.

Whatever the quality of their accommodation, food or medical care the gladiators were kept under lock and key and constantly watched by armed guards. No Roman wanted another Spartacus on his hands.

The training of a new recruit began with exercise at the *palus*, a thick wooden stake standing some six feet tall. The recruit was set to attack the pole, as if it were an opponent, with a variety of wooden weapons both offensive and defensive. The watching lanista would gauge his skill with the different fighting techniques needed by the different categories of gladiator. The recruit would then be assigned to the category of fighting that he would use for his career in the arena, however long that might last.

The recruit was next put under the authority of a doctor, or specialist trainer, who would teach him the techniques and fine points of using the weapons assigned to him. After a few weeks, the fledgling gladiator was issued with blunt, iron weapons. These were much heavier than the real steel versions used in the arena and were designed to build up strength and stamina. Real, sharp-edged weapons were kept in a locked storehouse some distance from the school so that gladiators were not tempted to try to kill their guards and escape.

The business of the doctors was not so much to teach the straightforward use of the weapons, but to instruct the recruits to use weapons in a way that would please the crowd. Hacking and slashing might kill a man, but it bored the mob. Gladiators were taught to use their weapons with ostentatious flourishes, building leaps and spins into their fighting movements. Some even juggled with their weapons in an attempt to please the crowd and thus win the missus in the event of losing the fight.

Apart from their armour, the gladiators usually fought and trained in their undergarments only. The Romans did not approve of nudity, which is why Greek style athletics were slow to become popular, but for gladiators there were two imperatives ruling their clothing and equipment. The first was that the crowd wanted to see blood. Unnecessary armour would have concealed the wounds and gore, which was hardly the way to please the audience. Additionally, fighting naked was a decided advantage to the gladiators. In the days before penicillin and other antibiotics, wounds were prone to fester and turn septic. Fragments of wool or linen that got caught in open wounds would only encourage infection.

As a result, the gladiators usually appeared in a version of the standard Roman man's underwear. This consisted of a large triangle of linen about 4 feet or so long on each edge. The cloth was tied around the waist so that two points met at the front and the third dangled down behind. This third point was then pulled up between the legs and tucked through the knot at the front. For ordinary Romans the cloth was made of plain, unbleached linen as it was rarely seen in public. For gladiators, however, the *subligaculum*, as it was known, was usually brightly coloured, edged with ribbon or heavily embroidered. Many gladiators secured the cloth with a thick belt around the waist. Made of tough leather and often decorated with embossed metal plates, the belt provided some protection to the abdomen.

After several months of training a novice gladiator would be put into the arena. Rarely did a complete beginner face a veteran: such a contest would have been over too quickly to win the editor favour with the crowd. Instead, novices fought each other on a one-to-one basis. Casualties in such combats were high. The untried gladiators lacked the defensive skills to ward off the potentially fatal blows to their torsos. Many were killed or mortally wounded in the arena. Even if they escaped serious injury, the newcomers were more likely to be voted death in the event of defeat. They did not have the necessary skills to impress the crowd and so win the missus. We know little about survival rates for novice gladiators, but they could not have been high.

For those who did live long enough to get experience the outlook was quite different. Grave stones and memorials erected to veteran gladiators make it clear that a good performer could expect to be granted the missus as often as the palm of victory in the later stages of his career. Not only did experienced fighters have the skills needed to impress the crowd, but they would also have teams of supporters, fan clubs in modern parlance. If their favoured man lost a fight, these supporters could be relied upon to set up the cry for the missus rather than see their hero die in the dust. One particularly successful gladiator, Flamma from Syria, fought thirty-eight times. Of these fights, Flamma won twenty-five bouts outright, was declared *stans missus* (a draw) nine times and lost four times, but won the missus. He retired from the arena at the age of thirty. Such a career was exceptional for the high proportion of wins.

A fact revealed by the career of Flamma, and the gravestone records of other gladiators was the number of fights in which they took part. Flamma was hired out for thirty-eight *munera* over a period of thirteen years, an average of one bloodthirsty performance every four months. This was about average for the first century AD. Later the fights became less frequent and the mortality rate higher. Clearly there was plenty of opportunity for training and exercise between bouts.

Successful gladiators such as Flamma received rewards for their efforts. The winner of each bout gained a palm branch to signify his victory and carried this in triumph around the arena after his fight. With the palms went the adulation of the crowd, which might have been useful if the gladiator lost his next fight.

Success in the ring could bring the gladiator a change of career. Many rich men hired gladiators to be their bodyguards or to guard their houses and valuables. Such employment was less hazardous than fighting in the arena and sometimes provided a route to life as a domestic slave.

Successful gladiators often became the centre of female adulation. Gangs of young girls would hang about the ludis hoping to catch a sight of their muscular hero, and even older women were not immune to the animal attractions of muscle, sweat and blood. The lanista was not above taking advantage of such infatuations. For a suitable fee a woman could spend the night with the gladiator of her choice. More than one woman bought a gladiator as a domestic slave to have him on hand for regular nights of passion. At least one even married her macho sex slave.

More practical than fame and women were the purses of money given to the winning gladiator. As a rule, the value of the winner's purse was agreed in advance between the editor of the games and the lanista of the gladiatorial troupe. If a gladiator put up a particularly skilful display the crowd might demand that he be given extra rewards, and the editor who wished to win favour with the crowd would be forced to put his hand in his pocket. The Emperor Claudius, when awarding extra money in this fashion, would hold up each gold coin in turn before dropping it into the hand of the gladiator. The crowd would enthusiastically count aloud as each coin fell.

The prize money given belonged to the gladiator to spend as he wished. Although a slave, a gladiator could own money and property.

Some chose to spend the money on drink, whores or other creature comforts. Some kept wives and handed their prize money over for the support of their families. For the criminals and freemen who were serving fixed terms as gladiators the cash benefits might be hoarded against their eventual release.

A few of the slave gladiators invested their money in the hope that one day they might be able to buy their freedom and escape from the arena. For these gladiators, however, there was a terrible dilemma. If they pleased the crowd, won victories and gained a mass of supporters they would win more and more money. But they would at the same time become increasingly valuable assets to the lanista. As they gained the means to buy their freedom they became too valuable to be able to afford themselves.

For such men there were a limited number of options. A greedy lanista might force them to continue fighting until they were killed. Other lanista might recognize that such highly skilled gladiators were worth more alive. They would be retained as doctors, or trainers, in the lanista's own ludis or hired out to other lanista to help teach their young fighters. Serious injury in the arena could also be a way out of the cycle of death. Gladiators without private money who were maimed or otherwise unable to fight might be kept by the lanista as cooks, cleaners or other staff around the ludis. Or they might be sold on to a private citizen eager to have a retired gladiator slave on hand to liven up dinner parties with tales of the arena.

The greatest prize any gladiator could receive was the *rudis*. This was a symbolic wooden sword, such as that used in training, which signified the gladiator was being set free from both the arena and from slavery. This was a sure way for an editor to win favour with the crowd. He could hire a particularly famous gladiator for the munus, then arrange in advance with the lanista to pay the price of the man's freedom. Come the big day the editor would set the gladiator free ostensibly as a prize for a magnificent fight. The adoring supporters of the gladiator would cheer the editor and, in all likelihood, vote for him at the next public elections.

For those who were able to buy their freedom or who won the rudis, retirement rarely marked the end of their gladiatorial career. Most of them had only one skill: fighting. They would take jobs as doctors in a ludis, often the one from which they had just been set free, or set up as teachers to give young noblemen lessons in self defence. Some freed gladiators set up their own ludis, training young men to become gladiators in their turn.

A few gladiators, having won their freedom, returned to the arena. It was usually cold, hard cash that tempted such men to risk their lives again. And editors were willing to pay huge sums of money, sometimes even offer entire country estates complete with slaves and farm equipment, to get famous gladiators back into the ring.

Such were the glittering prizes on offer to the gladiator who won both his fights and the support of the crowds. For the defeated who failed to impress there was only death. It was on this death that the whole edifice of gladiatorial display was ultimately built. For the defeated a quick, clean death was the best that could be expected. For the crowd an orgy of gore and blood was essential.

Gladiators were taught to kill and to die with stoicism. The defeated warrior who failed to gain the missus had a choice of deaths. He could kneel on the ground beside his opponent, leaning forward to grasp the man's left knee with his own left hand. This exposed the neck to his enemy. A swift, single cut to the throat severed the main arteries and ensured a swift, bloody death. If the defeated was too badly injured to get to his knees, he would be dispatched by a single thrust from behind which plunged a blade into his heart.

The dead man was then carried out of the arena and taken for burial. Often no gravestone was provided for those who died in the arena, though their fellow gladiators might club together to pay for some form of funeral.

The life of a gladiator offered glittering prizes, but most often it was painful, violent and short.

But for one particular class of gladiator the arena held little in the way of risk and virtually no danger. These men were exceptionally rare and it was a most unusual gladiatorial game which saw them fight in the arena. They were emperors.

For an emperor to set himself on a par with gladiators, among the most despised people in ancient society, seems bizarre. But the gladiators were also the objects of hero worship and had large followings of fans.

Most emperors stayed out of the arena, but those who ventured on to the sands may have done so to share some of the adulation given to the men of blood.

Certainly that is true of one of the emperors who entered the arena. Nero was always ready to sing, dance or act in front of an audience. His artistic gifts were real, but his thirst for applause was proverbial. In the mornings of *munera*, Nero liked to join the *venatores* to show off his skill with bow or spear. Usually he tackled nothing more dangerous than deer or hares, but these animals were fast and agile enough to show that Nero was genuinely good at hunting.

On one well known occasion, however, Nero tackled a lion when armed only with a single hunting spear. It was widely rumoured that the lion had been 'prepared' by the animal keepers by having its teeth pulled and its main muscles torn, though there was little sign of this in the arena. Nero did not repeat the stunt, so perhaps he had had a bit of a fright.

Nero's predecessor Caligula was more in the habit of frightening others than of being scared himself. Caligula delighted in bloodthirsty practical jokes. He would often joke to dinner guests about having poisoned their wine, and sometimes actually did so just to add grim humour to the situation. When one nobleman was about to be thrown to the wild beasts in the arena, he screamed loudly at Caligula for mercy. The emperor had the man brought up to the Imperial seat as if to grant mercy, then killed him.

The young emperor was not just bloodthirsty, he was also genuinely skilled at arms. He had grown up in the army camps where his father was a general and had earned the nickname Caligula, which meant 'Little Boots' from the soldiers. As an adult, Caligula trained assiduously with arms. This was standard practice for Roman noblemen and the emperor was not alone in hiring gladiators to teach him the finer points of swordsmanship. Nor was he alone in preferring Thracian style gladiators, for most men had their favoured style of fighter.

Where Caligula was unusual was in donning the equipment of a Thracian and appearing in the arena itself. Caligula sometimes appeared anonymously behind the closed visor of the helmet, but at other times had himself announced. Some of his bouts were display fights against famous gladiators, others were little more than executions when he fought condemned men armed with blunt weapons.

A similar pattern was followed by the otherwise quite sensible emperor Hadrian who liked to show off his undoubted skill with weapons. He fought animals, as had Nero, or indulged in display bouts as did Caligula. Other emperors showed off their skills in the arena by shooting at targets or killing animals.

In a quite different league altogether was Commodus, emperor from AD 180 to 192. Commodus inherited power from his father, Marcus Aurelius, at the age of just eighteen. From the start, he preferred to leave the actual day to day running of the Empire to his staff and, on the whole, he chose these men wisely.

Commodus was a tall, muscular man and had a very real skill with weapons. At first he went into the arena to show off his talents in relatively harmless fashion. One chronicler recorded 'His marksmanship with a bow was generally agreed to be astonishing. On one occasion he used some arrows with crescent-shaped heads to shoot at ostriches. Commodus decapitated the birds at the top of their necks with his arrows so that they went on running around as though they had not been touched.'

Another contemporary wrote 'On one day he killed a hundred bears all by himself, shooting down at them from the railing of the balustrade. On other days he would go down to the arena and cut down all the animals that approached him. He also killed a tiger, a hippopotamus and an elephant.'

The young emperor also engaged in display bouts with famous gladiators: 'In the afternoon he would fight as a gladiator. The form of contest that he practised and the armour that he used were those of the *secutores*. He held the shield in his right hand and the wooden sword in his left. Indeed, he took great pride in the fact that he was left-handed.'

After ten years in power, however, something happened to Commodus. He began to interfere in the running of the government and ordered the execution of loyal servants on apparently trivial grounds. He also began to kill in the arena in earnest. His opponents were still given wooden swords and told they were to take part in display fights, but Commodus used real weapons and killed them.

Commodus also took part in the execution of criminals. He liked to compare himself to Hercules and would appear at parties dressed as the ancient hero in a lionskin cloak and carrying a huge club. It was in this guise that he took part in executions, using his club to smash open the skulls of the condemned.

During the November games of AD 192 Commodus dispatched an opponent, then picked up the severed head and waved it at the seated Senators. He gave them a grim smile. He was, in fact, planning to make the surprise execution of the two Consuls of Rome the highlight of the next games. When the commander of the Praetorian Guard learned of these plans he feared that he would be next to die and he organized the murder of the emperor.

After the excesses of Commodus, few emperors went into the arena. The sands were left to the professionals.

V

، VARIETIES OF KILLER ،

THROUGHOUT THE SEVEN CENTURIES during which gladiators fought in Rome there were changing fashions in equipment, armour and fighting methods. Some of these were popular for only a short time, others persisted for generations. All the ways of fighting and types of equipment were designed to thrill the audience and make the games as spectacular as possible. Their usefulness to the gladiators themselves was at best incidental.

Whatever the type of gladiator, the design of their armour followed a general pattern. The head and neck were usually heavily protected by metal helmets which would have been proof against almost any weapon used in the arena. The legs were protected by metal greaves on the shins and often by leather or fabric padding on the thighs. The arms were also protected by armour of one sort or another. The body, however, was generally left bare. This is in direct contrast to the usage of armies throughout the pre-firearms age. Soldiers tended to wear armour that protected their bodies, while often leaving the limbs unarmoured.

The way in which gladiator armour was set out shows the demands of the games. The audience wanted to witness a thrilling combat between skilled fighters and expected it to last for some time. Fights are thought to have gone on for fifteen or twenty minutes as three or four combats to the hour seems to have been normal.

Such a contest was unlikely if the legs or arms were vulnerable to

GLADIATORIAL SCENES

Top: the mosaic shows *secutor* gladiators, armed with short swords, defeating a *provocator* (top left), and a *retiarius* (bottom left). To the right stands the figure of an amoured murmillo.

Above: the figure battling the leopard on the lower right is a *hoplomachus*, armed with a 6-foot spear.

Left: a Roman stone carving of a *secutor* (left) and a *retiarius*.

weapons. A quick stab to the opponent's sword arm could have rendered him incapable of carrying on the fight but would not necessarily have caused serious damage nor put his life at risk. It was to avoid these minor but disabling injuries that the armour to the arms and legs was used. Leaving the torso unarmoured, however, made this the obvious target for an attacking gladiator. Hitting the torso is more difficult than striking the limbs. To make a hit would have required a lot of skill. Also desirably, from the Roman point of view, a blow to the torso was life-threatening and would certainly have ensured plenty of blood flow from a wound.

By keeping the limbs covered and the torso exposed, gladiators were encouraged to put on the type of show the crowd wanted to watch. High levels of skill would necessarily have been on display because the unskilled gladiators would have been dead. Combats were unlikely to have been cut short by a chance wound to a limb and so would have lasted long enough for the audience to be satisfied. And, when a wound was inflicted, the crowd had the added excitement of seeing plenty of blood and knowing the wound might prove fatal.

The armour made for the gladiators was special not just in its distribution on the body but also in the way it was designed. In theory many gladiators wore armour and carried arms based on those of distinct nationalities, such as Samnites, Gauls or Thracians. In fact the equipment was exaggerated for effect and often decorated with excessively showy plumes and crests that would not have been used by real soldiers.

The metal armour was also relatively heavy and robust. Archeological finds of gladiatorial armour shows that the helmets were made of bronze, often plated with tin or even gold. The metal had an average thickness of about 1.5mm and the complete helmets weighed from six pounds up to fifteen pounds. This made the helmets about twice as heavy as the helmet of a Roman legionary of the period.

Leg greaves and arm protectors were likewise stronger and heavier than their military counterparts. The extra weight was made possible by the fact that gladiators did not wear their armour for very long. Soldiers on the march in hostile territory might keep their armour on for hours each day, for day after day. Gladiators by contrast would don their fighting equipment just before entering the arena and, if they lived, take it off some twenty or thirty minutes later.

It is worth noting that all later forms of gladiatorial helmet had full face visors. These were sometimes made up of metal grills through which the wearer could see and breathe, or were solid sheets punctured by holes, but all forms hid the face of the fighter. These helmets came into use about AD 20, the earlier gladiators using open face helmets. The visors were hinged at the side, opening outwards like a pair of gates. The visors gave protection to the face and neck, but they also served to dehumanize the fighter. With his face covered and invisible, the gladiator became impersonal. No doubt this helped when a gladiator was set to fight a colleague from his own barracks. Even the most hardened gladiator might have felt rather inhibited when it came to killing a mate.

In addition to the metal armour, gladiators wore a variety of leather and cloth protective gear. The most common of these were tubes of heavy quilting worn over the lower legs or the sword arm. Made up of layer upon layer of wool or linen fastened in place with leather straps, these *fasciae* provided protection against the relatively light weapons used in the arena. Metal greaves were sometimes fitted over the quilting for added protection, and also to allow for decorative metal embossing.

Gladiators seem to have fought barefoot at all times. Presumably this gave a better grip in the sand on which they trod.

The following categories of gladiator are identified largely by their arms and armour. We know what these types of fighter wore and which weapons they used. There are dozens of depictions of the various categories on vases, lamps and in the form of small statuettes. What is rather less certain is the fighting method adopted by each category of killer.

There are a few written references to men known as *summa rudis*, who acted as referees during gladiatorial combats. This would imply that there were rules to be enforced and that the fights were not totally no-holds-barred in nature. If a shield or piece of armour broke or fell free, for instance, the summa rudis would declare a *diludium*, or temporary halt in the fight so that armourers could come on to repair the damage. In some combats one of the fighters was placed on a mock bridge which the opponent had to fight his way across. Other fights took place with one of the combatants on a pedestal. There were also fights which involved lines of chalk being laid down on the sand. The precise rules of these fights are unknown, but rules there clearly were.

The summa rudis had another duty as well. They would shout advice and instructions to the gladiators, on attack and defence. If the gladiator did not follow instructions or was considered not to be showing the necessary degree of aggression, the summa rudis could interrupt the fight to administer a flogging.

The earliest gladiators fought with weapons from the standard Roman military armoury. The first distinctly different category of gladiator was the Samnite. These men appeared in the arenas as prisoners of war taken from the Samnite peoples of central eastern Italy. They were originally dressed in typical equipment of the Samnite army, most noticeably a large shield and ostentatiously showy helmet with a variety of plumes and crests. Soon after the Samnites, the Gauls started to appear in the arena. Again these men were originally prisoners of war taken from the Celtic tribes of Gaul. By about 70 BC these two had been joined by a third type of gladiator based on a foreign national army, the Thracian.

By about AD 50 the various types of gladiator had become formalized with standard weapons and armour. It had also become customary to pitch a fighter of one type against a specific type of opponent. The balancing of advantages and disadvantages between the opponents was a key consideration when organising a gladiatorial contest.

Often the first to take to the arena were the *equites*, gladiators who fought on horseback. These men were armed with weapons typical of Roman cavalry of around 100 BC. They wore simple tunics which lacked sleeves and had a broad stripe of colour running from shoulder to hem on either side of the body. The lower legs were protected by quilted armour, as was the right arm. The left arm carried a small round shield. The helmet was a simple round skull cap with a metal brim attached. The brim was straight at the front and sides, but often swept down at the back to protect the nape of the neck. The face was, as usual covered by a hinged visor.

For weapons the equites had long lances and short swords. The lances were about seven feet long and ended in a broad, leaf-shaped point. The swords were the standard infantry sword, the gladius, of the Roman army.

The equites entered the arena on horseback, grey stallions being the preferred mount. At some stage in the fight the men dismounted to continue on foot. The precise reason for this is not clear, but as the pictures showing them on foot have them fighting with swords alone it may have been that the men dismounted if their lances broke. Whatever the rules governing the equites may have been, they usually seem to have ended up off their horses and on their feet.

About AD 30 the Samnite class of gladiator seems to have fallen out of favour and been replaced with the *murmillo*, who was nevertheless equipped in much the same way. The murmillo wore a helmet with a wide flat brim which was topped by a large, upright metal crest to which could be fixed feathers or a horsehair crest. The name murmillo is derived from the Greek word for a type of fish, the large crest perhaps indicating a dorsal fin. Some helmets were etched with depictions of fish scales and may have been embellished with tin or gold plate. In the sunlight these helmets would have been a spectacular shimmering sight.

The murmillo carried a large rectangular shield very like that of the Roman legionary, being over three feet high and about two feet across. The shield was made of layer upon layer of thin wood glued together and pressed into a mould to give a semi cylindrical shape. The edges of the shield and the central boss were reinforced with sheet bronze. The face of the shield was covered in leather and painted with a variety of colourful designs. On his left arm the murmillo wore a stout metal greave over quilted padding. The sword arm was sheathed in quilted padding from shoulder to the wrist, the hand being protected by the sword hilt. In all he carried about forty pounds of equipment, some eighteen pounds of which was the shield.

The stance taken by a murmillo is shown on many mosaics and pictures. The fighter stood side on to the enemy with his left side advanced. He crouched slightly so that the long shield protected the body completely from the bottom of the helmet visor to the top of the greave. In this position his entire body was protected from attack.

The murmillo was most often put to fight a gladiator of either the Thracian or the *hoplomachus* category, both being rather more lightly armed than the murmillo.

The Thracian carried a formalized version of the traditional weapons of the warriors of Thrace, a country today mostly in the territory of

Bulgaria. The distinctive feature of the Thracian outfit was a curved helmet crest which carried an ornamental griffin. Some helmets had cups in which could be mounted long feathers, but the helmet was unadorned by large crests, the fearsome griffin sculpture being thought decoration enough. The griffin was considered sacred to Nemesis, the goddess of revenge, which probably explains why it supplanted the wide variety of animals featured on earlier Thracian helmets.

The shield carried by the Thracian was a square about two feet along each side. Made from laminated wood, the shield had a large metal boss which could be used to punch at the opponent. The smaller size of the shield meant that the greaves needed to be longer. Usually a greave was worn on each leg and they reached from the ankle to above the knees. The thighs were covered in quilted padding, as was the sword arm, to protect against sword thrusts.

The Thracian was a more mobile fighter than the murmillo. He was expected to use fancy footwork to back away from or to dart into the attack. His lighter equipment made more nimble movements possible, while the small shield made them essential.

To inflict injury upon his opponent, the Thracian had a short, curved sword which could be used to slash, but more often in the arena was for stabbing. The native Thracian weapon had a gentle curve rather like a sickle, but a later variant was made up of an almost straight blade which bent sharply halfway along its length.

Similar in some ways to the Thracian, and also often pitched against the murmillo, was the hoplomachus. This variety of gladiator was derived from the heavily armed *hoplite* of Greek armies. He wore a Greek style helmet and carried a Greek type round shield, though it was much smaller than that of a true hoplite, being only about eighteen inches in diameter. It was made of a thick sheet of bronze and was deeply dished. It was heavy and could be a formidable weapon in its own right. Like the Thracian, the hoplomachus wore long metal greaves over extensive quilted padding on the legs.

For a weapon the hoplomachus had a spear about six feet long. This gave the man a greater reach than other gladiators. No doubt this was combined with his lighter armour to create a fluid, more dynamic style of fighting. If the spear was broken, the hoplomachus had a short dagger to use as a final weapon. The combination of spear and dagger is typical of Greek infantry in the first century BC, when Rome was fighting the various Greek states.

It seems likely that the pitching of a murmillo, equipped in a version of Roman equipment against the Thracian or hoplomachus was designed to recreate a stylized version of combats between the Romans and their foreign enemies which had happened many times on the battlefields.

That is not the case with the *provocator*, a class of gladiator that originated in the first century BC and remained popular thereafter. These men usually fought against other provocators rather than against different types of gladiator. The provocator, like the murmillo, carried a legionary-style shield, short greaves and quilted sword arm armour. He was equipped with a short, stabbing sword. The helmet shape was unique as it lacked a brim or a crest. The smooth bowl for the helmet was hammered from a single sheet of bronze and reached down to the back of the neck. The face was, as usual, covered by a pierced visor.

Unlike most other gladiators, the provocators had partial body armour. They wore a small breastplate which covered the upper part of the chest and was secured in position by leather straps which crossed over behind the back. These heavily armed men would have engaged in fairly static sword fights in which skill with the shield would have been paramount.

Towards the end of the first century AD an entirely new form of gladiator became popular. Unlike the other types of arena fighter the format of the *retiarius* was not based upon any real soldier. Instead he seems to have come from a marine environment, though it is entirely obscure how the combination of arms and armour seen in the gladiatorial version came about.

The retiarius had no shield, no helmet and no greaves. His defensive armour consisted solely of quilted padding on the left arm and a metal shoulder plate which gave some protection to the upper arm, shoulder and left side of the neck. After the second century AD, the retiarius sometimes carried a sleeve of mail on his left arm, which continued across his chest.

The offensive equipment of the retiarius consisted of a long trident with a stout wooden handle and wickedly sharp prongs. He also carried a circular fishing net which was tied to his left wrist by long strings. The retiarius was the most lightly armed of all the gladiators, relying on speed and dexterity for defence rather than on armour. He attacked by casting his net in the hope of entangling his opponent, and then stabbing him with the trident. If the net got caught by the other gladiator, the retiarius had a short knife to cut himself free.

Facing the light, nimble retiarius was the much more heavily armed *secutor*. In many ways the secutor was armed as a murmillo, but with adaptations to make him more suitable for facing the retiarius. The flamboyant crests and ornamentation of the murmillo helmet would have become easily entangled in the net of the retiarius, so the secutor's helmet was perfectly smooth. The flanges were also smooth and resembled fish fins, most appropriate for a fighter facing a man with a net. The open grill that formed the visor of the murmillo's helmet would also have been a disadvantage against a retiarius as it would have allowed through stabs from the sharp trident. So the secutor helmet had a visor made of solid metal in which were pierced two small eye holes. The field of vision was remarkably small, but the eyes and face were protected.

The very different fighting styles of the lightly armed retiarius and the heavily armoured secutor proved to be enduringly popular with the Roman crowd. The secutor tried to close quickly with the retiarius to use his superior weight at close quarters. The retiarius did his best either to entangle the other gladiator in the net and bring him to the ground or to extend the battle until the secutor tired under the weight of his armour.

The fact that the retiarius alone fought without his face covered meant that the *lanista* would often choose the best looking among his fighters to play this role. These men became favourites with the women, though their habit of running away led to some derisive comments from men. Some slurs about the pretty boy nature of the retiarius were made throughout their time in the arena. They seem to have been treated as the lowest of the low by other gladiators, though it is not easy to understand the contempt in which the net fighters were held.

The categories of gladiator described so far were the most popular in the Roman arena. They appeared at games after games for centuries and continued to fight right up to the demise of the gladiatorial games. But there were other types of gladiator who appeared from time to time, or in small numbers.

When the Emperor Claudius returned to Rome after invading Britain in AD 43 he brought back many prisoners of war to fight for the entertainment of the Roman citizens. Among them were some British warriors highly skilled at fighting from war chariots. These chariots were two-wheeled vehicles pulled by a pair of hardy mountain ponies. The chariot carried a driver and a warrior. The chariots would be driven into the arena at full speed to wheel and manoeuvre at the gallop while the warriors threw spears at each other. The dexterity of some fighters was such that they could run out on to the pole between the two ponies to throw their spears forward.

As with the *equites*, the charioteers seem to have usually dismounted at some stage in the contest. They then fought on foot with oval, British style shields and fairly long swords. It is unclear at which point in the fight the men climbed down from the chariots, but the moment was certainly understood by those watching. The charioteers did not remain in service for long, perhaps because of the cost of the chariots and the difficulty of finding skilled drivers.

Similarly short lived in popularity were the archers based on troop types of the Empire's eastern neighbours. These men appear to have worn quite heavy armour and to have used powerful curved bows. How they fought each other is unknown, but they feature often enough in pictures and mosaics to indicate that they must have been fairly prominent even if only for a short period of time.

The *paegniarius* were a form of grotesque clown who appeared at gladiatorial games. They were dressed in imitation gladiator armour, often with humorous or erotic designs on their shields or with bizarre decoration on their armour. They came on to caper about to entertain the crowd while scenery was being changed or gladiators were preparing to fight in earnest. Most of the paegniarius seem to have indulged in jokey antics designed to parody the more serious fighting techniques of the true gladiators, but they sometimes made caustic reference to topical events or staged supposed recreations of mythical events, such as duels between cupids and satyrs.

There are other types of gladiators on record about which relatively little is known. The *laquerarius* was armed with a lasso and may have been a specialized type of retiarius. The *dimarchaeri* were armed with two swords but no shields. The bizarre *andabatae* were horsemen dressed in heavy chain mail who wore helmets lacking any eyeholes at all. Presumably they slashed blindly at each other using the sounds of the other's mount to try to locate him.

One novelty that was popular for a while was the introduction of women gladiators. These women were generally put into combat only against other women. The staging of a fight against a man would have been considered rather unfair. The women gladiators appear to have fought in a modified form of murmillo armour. They had the large shield and short sword, but lacked the helmet. Presumably they were left bare headed so that the crowd could see that they were women. The chest was modestly covered by fabric, though it is not clear if this was a simple tunic or a form of padded armour.

Female gladiators never appeared in large numbers and may have been part of the humorous paegniarius more often than part of the bloody gladiatorial fighting. In AD 200 the Emperor Septimius Severus banned women from appearing in the arena in any role at all.

These were the styles of combat and of fighting that dominated the arenas of blood for centuries. But it was not just as gladiatorial single combat that blood was shed on the sands of the arena. The Romans were nothing if not inventive when it came to killing their fellow humans.

The most elaborate and expensive of all the spectacles of Rome were the naval combats staged between real warships on lakes or artificial bodies of water. The great naval fight staged by the Emperor Claudius took place on Lake Fucino and saw the deaths of hundreds of men by swordplay or drowning. The Emperor Nero adapted the Coloseum so that it could be flooded to hold his own naval battles.

VI

˒ THE NAVAL BATTLES ˒

WHILE THE GLADIATORS were fighting each other in armour largely based on the military equipment of Rome and her enemies, ambitious politicians seeking new and more ostentatious entertainments for the mob turned to the naval wars for inspiration. The results were the *naumachiae*, imitation naval battles which were perhaps the most expensive and unusual of all the games staged by the Romans.

The first naumachia to be staged for the entertainment of the crowd was put on by Julius Caesar during his great games of 46 BC. At the time Caesar had just completed a ruthless grab for dictatorial power by executing hundreds of rival nobles and defeating armies led by his rival Gnaeus Pompey, also executed. The purpose of the games was to ensure Caesar's popularity with the Roman mob and so make his new regime secure. In addition to gladiatorial combats, plays, free banquets and other entertainments, Caesar announced he was to stage a naval battle. The spectacle was to include over a dozen ships and 3,000 men.

To accommodate the coming battle, Caesar set an army of workmen to the task of excavating an artificial lake on the Campus Martius, the Field of Mars. This was a large area of flat land just north of the city walls which was used for army training and manoeuvres. The lake was only a few feet deep as the warships of the time had very shallow draughts, but it covered a vast expanse, perhaps 400 yards square.

The fight, Caesar announced, was to recreate an historical battle between Egypt and Tyre. It was an inspired choice. In the wars just completed the ancient and splendid port of Tyre had been secured as part of the Roman Empire. Egypt, although still independent, had become a satellite of Rome after Caesar intervened in a civil war to place the youthful Queen Cleopatra VII on the throne. Both places were, therefore, very much in the news as far as the Roman public was concerned. The proposed scenario was even more topical as the new Queen of Egypt had recently arrived in Rome on an official visit, bringing with her the baby boy who was her son by Caesar himself.

The naval battle Caesar was proposing to recreate had taken place some centuries earlier. At that time the Tyrians would have been equipped with high-sided ships powered by two banks of oars. The main weapon of the ships was a sharp ram located just beneath the surface at the front. The captains aimed to ram and sink an enemy ship, though there were armed soldiers to board an enemy vessel if necessary. The Egyptian ships of the period relied almost exclusively on boarding for victory, but their design is little known.

It is most likely that Caesar did not attempt historical accuracy when it came to the design of the ships. Given the numbers involved, Caesar probably provided ships similar to the liburnian galley which was the standard ship of the Roman navy in home waters.

The liburnian was a bireme, having two banks of oars one each side, which provided sixty oars along each side with a single rower operating each oar. The ship sat low in the water and had a fairly broad beam. The overall width of the ship was about fifteen feet and its length was around 110 feet. Like the earlier Tyrians' ships, the liburnian had a pointed ram just below water level projecting from the bows. Captains would attempt to ram an enemy ship in the flanks, using the ram to smash a hole in the enemy planking and cause the ship to sink. Liburnians also carried a force of forty armed soldiers who gathered on platforms at the front or rear of the ship ready to hurl themselves on board the enemy if this was felt to be a better tactic. These front and rear platforms were connected by a walkway running down the centre of the ship, between the banks of rowers. Caesar provided some smaller ships for his staged naval battle, but details of these are lacking.

The excitement generated by the naumachia was immense and vast crowds flocked to the Campus Martius to watch the entertainment. Some camped out on the open ground beforehand so that they could get good viewpoints from which to watch the coming battle. On the day itself, the crowds were so great that several people were crushed to death, including two senators.

It is unfortunate that we have no records of how Caesar recruited the 3,000 men who took part in his naval battle. One witness states that there was much in the way of skilful manoeuvring and clever tactics, but makes little mention of actual bloodshed. It took some months to train rowers to handle the long, heavy oars which powered these craft. To get 100 or more men to row in perfect unison to a steady beat was difficult enough. To train them to be able to back water suddenly on both sides of the ship or on one side only, to change rowing speed instantly or to reverse in seconds took many weeks of hard effort. If the ships were handled with the skill that is reported, the crews would have been trained naval personnel. Caesar's recent wars had been against armies, not naval enemies, so there would have been no supply of prisoners of war whom Caesar could send to their deaths. It is possible that Caesar's naval battle was more of a spectacle than a bloodbath.

We know rather more about a naumachia held by Augustus in 2 BC. The occasion for the event was the dedication of the Temple of Mars the Avenger which had been built in honour of Julius Caesar, Augustus' uncle. Caesar's artificial lake on the Campus Martius had been filled in a few years after the earlier naval battle when its waters turned stagnant. Augustus ordered the building of a new lake, this time on the banks of the River Tiber, in the area now known as Trastevere. The artificial lake was about 600 yards by 400 yards and was fed by an aqueduct bringing fresh water from a spring over fifteen miles away. With more of an eye to the long term than his uncle, Augustus had the lake built so that it would serve as a reservoir for the city when not in use for spectacles.

Like Caesar, Augustus announced that the coming battle was to be a recreation of an historic event. Augustus chose a naval battle between Athenians and Persians as his theme. Greek culture was fashionable in Rome at the time, so the spectacle was no doubt intended to cash in on the current vogue. Again there seems to have been little attempt at historical accuracy. The ships were of contemporary Roman patterns, and did not resemble the sleek triremes that the Greeks had used during the Persian Wars nearly four centuries earlier. The only concession to reality was that the 'Persian' ships were gaudily painted to conform with Roman stereotypes of Eastern magnificence. In all the battle featured thirty ships, presumably with fifteen on each side.

Nor does there seem to have been much sign of the skilful naval manoeuvres displayed by Caesar's spectacle. Indeed, Augustus issued strict orders that this battle was to be fought and won by boarding tactics. To make the battle as real as possible and to bring a touch of gladiatorial bloodshed to the proceedings, Augustus put 5,000 gladiators on his ships, in addition to the rowers. The rowing crews may have been naval personnel whose task was to get the ships into position so that the gladiators could do their bloody work. Five thousand was a very large number of men to send into deadly combat even by the standards of ancient Rome. It is probable that most of the fighters were condemned criminals. Those who died were seen as being executed, those who survived had won their lives though they remained criminals and probably were used as slaves.

For the Romans watching this enormous display, the social side of the event made as much impression as the ships and dying men. One poet celebrated the fact that people poured into the city from far and wide to watch the naumachia:

> From every land fair maidens came
> And youths from every sea around
> Abundant fuel for love's flame
> When all the world in Rome was found.
> Each man's heart was in a awhile
> Enraptured by some foreign girl.

The juxtaposition of the large scale bloodshed and suffering for the hapless combatants next to a spot of idle romance may be shocking to modern readers. The Romans seem to have thought it all perfectly normal.

Although they were hugely expensive, the naumachiae proved to be so popular that the emperors felt that they had to stage them from time to time. The Emperor Claudius decided to use a naumachia to celebrate the greatest engineering work of his time in power. For years he had employed workmen in tunnelling a channel from Lake Fucino, some miles east of Rome, to the nearby River Liris. The draining of the lake would open up a large area of marshland and bog to agriculture, and allow the water to be used to irrigate the nearby plain. This was certainly a feat to be commemorated.

Claudius followed his predecessors by announcing that he was recreating a real battle, that between Rhodes and Sicily. But he outdid the earlier battle displays by the sheer scale of the event and the killing. No fewer than 19,000 condemned prisoners were mustered to take part. They were given some rudimentary training in naval matters beforehand and supplied with ships built cheaply of unseasoned timber on which to fight. Neither the men nor the ships were expected to last very long. For security purposes, Claudius mustered an army of regular soldiers which lined the shores of the lake with drawn weapons to cut down any criminals who tried to escape. The army was equipped with large catapults to sink any ship which threatened to break away from the battle.

As news of the forthcoming vast spectacle spread, crowds began to gather. On the day of the battle itself the slopes around Lake Fucino were thronged with hundreds of thousands of spectators who had come from all over Italy to watch. Claudius appeared on the Imperial dais dressed in a beautifully embroidered military cloak. Beside him sat his wife Agrippina wearing a dress made of cloth of gold.

As the doomed convicts were marched down to their ships, they turned to face Claudius raised their arms and gave the traditional salute *Ave Caesar morituri te salutant*, meaning 'Hail, Caesar, we who are about to die salute you.' Claudius leaned forward and shouted back 'Well, perhaps not', which was not the standard reply. The convicts took Claudius' remark to mean that they had been spared from death and promptly refused to board their ships.

Claudius was furious and sent for the armed soldiers to force the prisoners on board. Still the men refused. The officer in charge was about to start executing the criminals, but Claudius again intervened. He realized that the vast crowd of people had come to see a naval battle, not merely the mass executions of prisoners. Claudius hurried down to the dockside and promised the reluctant fighters that if the battle went ahead as planned the winners would not just save their lives but would actually be set free. Only then did the prisoners take their places and row their ships out on to the lake.

Claudius went back to his dais and gave the signal for the battle to begin. As if by magic a silver triton emerged from the waters of the lake and blew his horn. In itself this was a mechanical marvel worthy of comment. No record was made of how the statue was made to rise from the waters, though presumably some mechanism of levers was involved. Once the beautifully shaped Triton with its fish tail and human body had blown the start signal on a giant shell, it was once again pulled back under the waters.

The battle that followed was fought with an unexpected zeal and ferocity. This delighted the crowd as they watched ships sinking, men drowning and boarding parties hacking each other to pieces. Finally the triton rose again to call for an end to the fighting. Claudius gave a signal for the water gates to be opened and the draining of the lake to begin.

Unfortunately things went wrong again. At first the power of the unleashed waters was so great that it swept away nearby jetties, podiums and men with great force. Then it was realized the lake was deeper than had been expected by the people responsible for draining it. Only part of it was emptied. Claudius was deeply annoyed and stormed back to Rome.

Perhaps because of the embarrassments surrounding the naumachia at Lake Fucino, the naval battles were thereafter held in conditions of much stricter control in Rome itself. In AD 57 Nero built a new wooden amphitheatre on the Campus Martius. Eager to impress the Romans, the emperor had the structure equipped with a complex set of water pipes so that the arena could be flooded or drained in just a few minutes.

On the main day of his games, Nero amazed and impressed the crowd by holding a wild animal hunt in his amphitheatre, then flooding it for a naumachia. He used miniature ships crewed by a handful of men but the battle was no less real or bloody as a result. As soon as the naval event was over, the drainage pipes were opened and the water gushed out of the arena. A few minutes later the newly revealed dry land was used for more spectacles.

This alternation of water and dry land proved to be very popular. In

AD 80 the Emperor Titus repeated the trick for the inaugural games at the Colosseum. The poet Martial recorded the excitement of the crowd:

> *There was land until a second ago*
> *Do you doubt it?*
> *Wait until the water drains away*
> *When the combat ends*
> *It will happen right away.*
> *Then you will say*
> *'the sea was there a moment ago'.*

Titus died of fever at the age of forty-two, and his younger brother Domitian came to power. Although an able administrator, Domitian had a volatile temper and could be quite arbitrary. In AD 84 Domitian held a naumachia on the reservoir built by Augustus for his naval games. As the battle raged a sudden storm swept down on Rome. Two of the ships capsized, drowning their crews, while bitterly cold winds and heavy rain lashed the audience. Domitian pulled a thick woollen cloak over his shoulders and ordered the battle to continue. The audience was forbidden to leave and forced to keep their seats. Finally the storm passed, but the audience were drenched to the skin. It was said that for some weeks afterward all Rome was ill, and many people died from the fevers they had caught. Suddenly remorseful, Domitian laid on a free banquet.

Despite the huge popularity of the naumachiae, they do not seem to have been a regular feature after the games of Domitian. There are scattered references to naval gladiators, but the large scale recreation of naval battles was abandoned by about AD 100. It may have been that the cost of the events in terms of money and life was simply too great. The crowds could apparently be satisfied with cheaper events and spectacles. There was no point in an emperor spending money if he did not need to.

Only once again was a naumachia to be held in Rome. In AD 248 the emperor Philip the Arab presided over the events celebrating the 1,000th anniversary of the founding of Rome. Among the magnificent games held to mark this momentous event was a naumachia staged on an artificial lake dug upstream from that built by Augustus. Dubbed the Naumachia Vaticana, the site has given its name to the modern home of the Popes.

The mob had, meanwhile, found a new favourite game in their orgies of blood. Pitting man against man was no longer enough to keep the crowd entertained. Now it was the turn of the wild animals.

VII

˒ WILD ANIMAL HUNTS ˒

I T WAS THE GREAT WARS against Carthage that brought wild animals to Rome in large numbers. Victory in war against the dominant power of North Africa gave Rome an empire and a new form of entertainment: the *venatio*. The term is usually translated as 'wild animal hunt', but the venatio was much more than that. As usual when it came to games of bloodshed, the Romans were nothing if not inventive.

Carthage was the centre of an enormously powerful empire that controlled the maritime trade of the western Mediterranean. Carthaginians controlled this trade as much by sinking the ships of rivals as by their own marketing skills. By 264 BC the Carthaginians had used their commercial wealth to build an empire which embraced North Africa from the Atlantic coast to the Gulf of Sirte as well as southern Spain, Corsica, Sardinia, the Balaerics and western Sicily. As Rome grew in power in Italy, she concluded a series of three trading treaties with Carthage.

In 264 BC Rome took the side of the Sicilian city of Messana against her neighbour Syracuse, backed by Carthage. The small conflict grew into a major war which ended in 241 BC with Carthage ceding control of Sicily and Sardinia to Rome. In 218 BC Carthage attempted to win back her lost power and prestige by sending the brilliant young general Hannibal to invade Italy by way of Spain and France. Although he won a series of outstanding victories, which still feature in the teaching in military academies around the world, Hannibal was finally ground down by

Gladiators riding elephants and horses battle a bull in a Roman amphitheatre. This form of entertainment was to become increasingly popular with Roman crowds during the third and second centuries BC.

weight of Roman numbers. In 203 BC he was recalled to Carthage and in the following year Hannibal and the Carthaginian army were defeated at Zama, not far from the gates of his home city.

It was the victory at Zama that brought the venatio to Rome. The battle had been won by Publius Cornelius Scipio, an already popular general who had held political office. Aiming to continue his political career now that the war with Carthage was over, Scipio set out to dazzle the Roman crowd. He chose to do this by displaying to the public an assortment of African animals. He brought home a number of crocodiles, an elephant and assorted gazelles which were paraded through the Forum Romanum to the delight of the crowd. The idea was novel and that in itself made it popular.

Soon every victorious general brought back to Rome a selection of animals native to the lands in which they had been fighting. Soldiers on campaign had long written home with accounts of bizarre animals, now the Romans could see the beasts for themselves. Julius Caesar brought a giraffe to Rome, and won great acclaim as no giraffe had been seen in the city before.

It was not long, however, before the generals parading animals through the Forum found they had a problem. What were they to do with the animals once they had been displayed to the crowd. Most of them were expensive to keep in captivity and a few, such as lions, were dangerous. The answer was to include the wild animals in the bloody games of the arena. Exotic animals brought from far distant lands were to be killed for the delight of the mob.

At first the animal fights were fairly straightforward affairs. The hapless beast to be killed was chained to a ring set in the pavement of the Forum and then attacked by men armed with spears and, sometimes, assisted by dogs. By the time Sulla became dictator of Rome in 82 BC such a format had become stale. For his animal hunt, featuring beasts from what is now Turkey, Sulla erected tough wooden fences around an open area in the Forum. The animals were then let loose to be hunted down by packs of dogs and men with spears. When the Forum was too small for the proposed display, the event was moved to the Campus Martius, the open fields north of the city, where the Saepta, or voting enclosures, could double as animal pens.

In 79 BC Gnaeus Pompey organized a fight between war elephants from North Africa and tribesmen skilled in hunting the beasts. The hunt was held in the Circus Maximus, the chariot racing course which was large and surrounded by banks of seating. Although Pompey's spectacular almost went wrong when the maddened beasts tried to attack the crowd, elephants remained a favourite of the Roman mob.

By the time of Augustus, who took power in 31 BC, the venatio had become so popular that it was usually included as part of a *munus*, or gladiatorial show. The venatio was looked upon as something of a warm up act for the gladiators and was usually staged in the morning. One thing always leads to another and the use of powerful animals necessitated a change to the architecture of the arenas. While gladiators could be kept from attacking the crowd by discipline, more physical methods were needed to contain the wild animals. Fences and metal grilles were used at first, but later the arenas were sunk into the ground so that the floor was several feet below the level of the seats. The wall around the arena was made smooth so that there was no way an animal could clamber out to endanger the crowd.

Those in the arena were, of course, often in great danger. There were two distinct types of man involved with the venationes. The first and least important were the *bestiarii*. These were the men who looked after the animals in their cages, giving them food and clearing out the cages of droppings. In the arena the job of the bestiarii was to get the animals into position and prepare them for whatever event the editor of the games had devised. Many animals were understandably frightened by the shouts of the crowd and intimidated by the large area of bare sand. They cowered in their cages rather than leaping out to play the role designed for them. It was the task of the bestiarii to get the animals to perform. It could be dangerous work.

More skilled and better regarded were the *venatores*, the hunters. These were the men who performed with the animals. In the early days of the venatio, the venatores were very much looked down upon by the gladiators and other staff of the arena. By about AD 150, however, they were becoming more respected and played an increasingly important role in the games.

The actual performances of the venatio varied enormously. Some animals were so bizarre that they were taken around from town to town by their keepers and merely displayed in the arena. Other animals were used in novelty acts, such as horse races run between dwarves on ponies. Such parodies of more serious events were great favourites with the Romans, the more grotesque the display the better.

Some animals were highly trained performers. We know of an ape which was trained to drive a chariot pulled by camels and one frieze from Rome seems to show a group of apes eating a meal using fashionable furniture, crockery and dishes – a sort of chimpanzee's tea party. There are also records of baboons dressed up to look like historic and topical characters. Apes and dogs were trained to undertake all sorts of tricks for the delight of the crowd.

Rather more gruesome were the attempts to recreate the appearance of foreign lands, complete with their native animals. The Romans could see lions, tigers, antelope and deer in the menageries or in the arena, but a new thrill was to see the animals behave as they did in the wild. Sometimes a lion would be released into an arena which already contained half a dozen deer. The crowd would then settle back to watch the lion stalk his prey while the deer attempted to escape. The truly artistic venatores would first decorate the performance area with trees or bushes in tubs. These gave some cover to the prey animals and also served to make the scene more lifelike for the audience. Factual nature films are commonplace on modern televisions, but gory displays with real animals were the only way that the Romans had to see such 'natural' behaviour.

Records show that the otherwise predictable animal hunts could be enlivened by setting a hungry predator against a creature well able to defend itself. Lions or leopards might be set to hunting down boars or bulls, which were powerful and equipped with tusks or horns capable of inflicting serious injury.

Such displays were interesting, but more bloodthirsty encounters were engineered when two hungry predators were loosed into an arena containing a single prey animal. The hunters would first despatch the prey, then turn on each other to quarrel over the meal. Battles between big male lions were especially popular, but leopards, cheetahs or wolves were also set against each other. At least once a lion was set to fight a tiger.

The animals, of course, did not always perform to demand. The bestiarii then needed to take recourse to tricks of the trade to make the animals fight. Keeping carnivores hungry was a simple method of making them more ferocious in the arena, but would not work with herbivores no matter how strong they might be. Bulls, boars and stallions were frequently goaded with sharp sticks before being turned loose.

Rather more imaginative was the chaining together of two animals. When released into the arena, each creature would naturally try to break free from the chain linked to a metal collar around its neck. Pulling on the chain would, of course, antagonize the beast on the other end of the chain, which would respond angrily in turn. By this simple stratagem almost any two beasts could be made to fight each other.

The most bizarre pairings were set up so that the crowd could witness the relative fighting merits of widely different animals. We know of a lion set to fight a crocodile, a bear set on a python and a seal matched with a wolf. Some of the pairings were used so regularly that they developed into traditional parts of any public animal display. The bull chained to a bear was one of the most popular, as was a bull against a big cat, such as a lion or leopard.

Always in demand by the crowd were those fights involving the two largest animals of the arena, the rhinoceros and the elephant. The rhinoceros had a reputation of being difficult to work with. Left to itself, the average rhinoceros would lumber around amongst the potted plants looking for something to eat. Once provoked to anger, however, the rhinoceros was virtually unstoppable. Its unpredictable charges of huge power and unrivalled destructiveness were favourites with the crowd, though they can hardly have been popular with the unfortunate bestiarii who had the task of goading the rhinoceros to fury. The elephant was likewise unlikely to attack unless dangerously provoked. This difficulty was overcome by using trained war elephants. The riders of the war elephants drove them to attack the wild elephants which had been herded into the arena.

The elephants were not used just for killing and fighting. Some of the more highly trained animals performed tricks similar to those seen in modern circuses. They were taught to dance in time to music, to march in column and line like army soldiers and how to walk on tightropes.

These performing elephants were reckoned to have great intelligence and were highly prized. In the first century AD a story ran around Rome that after one performing elephant had put on a poor show it had been severely chastised by its trainer. That night, by the light of the moon, the elephant returned by itself to the training arena to practise its tricks time after time until it achieved perfection.

However, the elephant riders were merely one of the classes of specially trained men who appeared with the animals in the arena. By far the most popular and numerous were the *taurocentae*, the bullfighters. There was little in common between the Roman bullfighters and their modern Spanish counterparts. The modern bullfights place emphasis on skill, grace and elegance for the bullfighter and on courage and tenacity for the bull. For the Romans it was daring and danger that counted for most.

In many ways the displays by the taurocentae were more akin to the activities in modern rodeos than to the more bloodthirsty games of ancient days. But there was one key difference. The bulls being used were not the male domestic cattle of today. Aggressive as these bulls can be, and the Spanish fighting bulls are bred for that very quality, their ferocity pales beside that of the wild aurochs used by the Romans. This wild ancestor of European cattle was over ten feet long, equipped with wickedly sharp horns which curved forward over its face and was notoriously unpredictable and aggressive. The aurochs became extinct in the seventeenth century, but in Roman times were widespread across Europe.

Faced with this monstrous beast, the taurocentae went in for a variety of displays. The bulls were chased by men on horseback who attempted to attach ribbons or markers to the bulls' horns in a game of tag which had ever present danger. More daring were the riders, known as the *tauromachus*. These men rode small, nimble horses from which they goaded and teased the bulls, first chasing them at full gallop, then retreating at high speed, until the bulls were utterly exhausted. At that point the tauromachus would leap from his horse to grab the bull's horns and wrestle it to the ground.

Even more admired were the acrobatic men who faced the bulls on foot armed only with a wooden pole about eight feet long. These men would pole-vault over the back of the charging bull, skip aside as the bull rushed past and, on rare occasions, sit astride the bull. Sometimes straw-filled dummies were used to distract the bull or goad it into charging, and it is believed the dummies had other uses, but these are unclear.

The various stunts of the taurocentae were first performed under the rule of Julius Caesar in his magnificent games held to appease the mob after he took power as dictator. The bull fighters came from Thessaly, a part of northern Greece where grazing land was more extensive than elsewhere in Greek territory. It is likely that the Thessalians brought to Rome by Caesar were herders who had acquired their skills, as did cowboys of the American West, through their constant work with cattle. For over a century the taurocentae seem to have been exclusively from Thessaly, but after that other nationalities were trained in these exciting skills.

The mighty aurochs were not used solely to show off the tricks and talents of the taurocentae. They were also killed in the arena by men called *taurarii*. Like their colleagues, the taurarii might appear on horse-back or on foot. These men were almost invariably armed with a strong, stout spear, in contrast to the slender sword used by today's matadors. As with the hunting of animals by animals, the taurarii might hunt their bulls in a bare arena or in one decorated with trees and bushes. The technique seems to have been to tire the bull by goading it into ill judged charges that could be sidestepped, then to move in for the kill. Ideally the bull would be induced to charge one last time, the hunting spear would be braced against the ground and the beast would impale itself as it thundered towards its tormentor.

As with modern bullfighting, of course, the bull did not always come off worst. More than one ancient carving or mosaic shows a taurarii being tossed by a bull, or lying injured on the sand. Such human casualties seem to have been the exception rather than the rule, however, for it was displaying the skill of the hunter and the blood of the bull that was the object of these events.

The bulls were not the only animals hunted by humans in the arena. A wide variety of animals were brought to Rome to die before the crowds at the hands of the *venatores*, the hunters. Gazelles and ostriches came from Africa, deer and boar from Europe. Sometimes the animals were loosed in random groups but on other occasions real efforts were made to produce an animal hunt using only animals from a certain province. In this way the Roman mob was reminded of the power of their city and the vast extent of their empire. This device became increasingly common under the Emperors who sought to flatter the crowd into docile obedience rather than to court their active votes as had the politicians of the Republic.

Most popular with the crowd were the truly dangerous carnivores such as lions, leopards and tigers. Bears, boars and bulls were also capable of killing a man so they too were loudly applauded by the crowd. The less dangerous antelopes, deer, ostriches and giraffes were seen more as tests of the skill of the hunters than as providing any real excitement.

As with the gladiators, the venatores were equipped in fashions to please and amuse the crowd rather than to help them defeat the animals they were set against. Like gladiators the venatores were largely slaves and, since they did not attract the following of fans that successful gladiators could acquire, their lives were cheap. Most venatores were armed with spears and daggers, sometimes with a bow and arrows. They wore no armour and relied on their skill with their weapons and an ability to dodge aside to defend themselves.

Some of these lightly armoured men learnt some quite bizarre tricks to defeat their animal opponents. Several venatores could stun a bear with a single, massive punch delivered just above the ear. One performer was said to have been able to kill a lion with his bare hands. He would force the beasts mouth open with one hand, then plunge his arm down the creature's gullet and choke it. The mind boggles as to how such a skill could be acquired.

There were also various props available to the lightly equipped venatores. One of the most frequently used was the cochlea. This was a large wooden door mounted on a frame so that it could spin around, rather like a modern revolving door. The venatores could hide behind the cochlea to gain some respite from attack. More skilled fighters used the cochlea as a weapon. They would stand beside it until the beast against which they were set attacked, then slam the heavy wooden door into the beast to inflict injury.

There were also wooden barrels and wicker traps, rather like gigantic lobster pots, into which a hunter could dive if he got into trouble. The angry bear, lion or other animal would paw futilely at the barrel or contraption until it lost interest and wandered off. The hunter could then emerge and begin the chase all over again. Such refuges were, of course, only any use if the venatores could get to them in time. More than one hunter died a bloody death trying to reach the safety of a cochlea or barrel.

Yet other hunters were heavily armoured. Sometimes a gladiator, or at least a man equipped as a gladiator, would be put into the arena with the wild animals. With the benefit of a helmet and shield this man had some protection against the tearing teeth and the claws but with only his sword as a weapon he was at a disadvantage as he lacked the long reach of the men equipped with hunting spears.

Even more extreme in the balance of strengths were the men who fought the animals clad in suits of chain mail, similar to those worn by auxiliary infantry in the army. These men were given only small daggers even when facing ferocious lions or powerful bears. The advantage they had in terms of armour was offset by their lack of an effective weapon. As ever, the Romans were inventive when it came to death.

Some of these bloody encounters took place as single combats, a lone man against a lion for instance. Others were massed spectacles in which several hunters entered the arena together to take on dozens of animals. Greater numbers increased the dangers enormously as a hunter could be struck down from behind while concentrating on tackling the animal to his front.

Increasingly popular under the Emperors was the variant on the wild beast hunt that went by the name of *silvae*. In this spectacle efforts were made to recreate the natural habitat of the animals to be hunted. Boulders and rocks were brought to the arena to simulate desert, large ponds were dug to imitate swamps or bushes and trees put in place to imitate the forests which gave the silvae their name. The animals were then released into simulated forest, marsh or desert to be hunted down by the venatores.

The spectacle reached a climax in the time of the third century Emperor Probus. Hailing from the Danube provinces, Marcus Probus was a son of a non-aristocratic farming family and gained the Imperium after an impressive career in the army. Probus came to power at a time when civil wars and economic breakdown had led to some years of disorder and hardship. Being a country boy, Probus saw the answer to the empire's problems in terms of rebuilding the farms of the provinces.

Having crushed his rivals and secured peace on the borders, Probus turned his army to doing large scale public works. Marshes in the deltas of the Nile and Danube were drained and turned over to use as grain-fields. Scrubland in the Balkans was converted to vineyards. Forests in the north were cleared for grazing land. Probus took advantage of these works which made many animals homeless to put on spectacular silvae in Rome and in many provincial cities. Artificial Nile marshes were constructed and populated with crocodiles and hippopotamuses while forests were filled with bears and wolves. His most famous spectacle was put on in Rome in AD 281 when an entire German forest, complete with mature trees larger than any seen in Rome, was dragged from the far north to form the backdrop to a days-long hunt during which 300 bears, among other northern creatures, were finished off.

The Roman mob loved such shows, but the army was unimpressed by being put to work draining swamps and planting vines. In September 282 the Praetorian Guard, led by its commander Marcus Carus, organized a military coup and Probus was murdered. The days when public spectacles assured success to politicians and emperors were on the wane. It was military power that was becoming the controlling factor in Roman politics.

Perhaps because of the failure of Probus to hold on to power after his magnificent silvae of AD 281, the fashion for hugely elaborate animal hunts began to fade. The slaughter of animals in the arena continued, however, and on occasion totalled enormous numbers.

There is in Tripoli a mosaic dating to about AD 200 which shows various animal fights taking place. Included is a strange scene which has long puzzled historians. The scene shows a bull and a bear chained together and fighting each other. This would seem to be a fairly typical pairing of dangerous animals as so often staged in the arena. But in this mosaic there is also a man. The man is entirely naked. He is equipped with a long rod on which is mounted a hook with which he is undoing the catch on the chain connecting the two beasts. Quite what is going on here is difficult to understand. If the enraged beasts were unchained they might lose interest in each other and turn on the only other moving object in sight – the man who had unchained them. And the man has neither weapons nor armour to protect himself. It is possible that in this mosaic we are seeing one of the most cruel and horrific of the events in the arena. This man could have been one of the condemned criminals, the *noxii*.

VIII

ꞏ EXECUTIONS ꞏ

P ERHAPS THE MOST UNPLEASANT of all the events that took place in the Roman arena were the executions of the *noxii*, prisoners condemned to death by the magistrates. It is not just to modern sensibilities that the gruesome executions appear offensive; many Romans found them repellent. For these were not straightforward public executions by beheading or hanging. Every refinement of cruelty and agony of which the Roman mind was capable was brought to bear on the noxii. And the Roman mind could be most imaginative.

Public executions were nothing unusual in the ancient world. In most societies they continued until just two centuries ago and in some countries continue today. The death penalty has been, and remains in many countries, the ultimate sanction of the state judicial system. For those crimes judged by society to be so terrible that there is no hope of redemption for the guilty person and in those places where the punishment ethic is strong, death is the only appropriate penalty. For some people certain crimes are so awful that the perpetrator must be destroyed and must be seen to be destroyed. Public execution is felt to be the ultimate sanction of society on its most anti-social elements.

For the Romans it became a public spectacle.

The development of the punishments inflicted on the noxii is complex and not properly understood. For the educated Roman who wrote down accounts of the games and recorded histories of Rome the

The philosopher Seneca was one Roman who disapproved of public executions, deploring their effect on the watching populace. Ironically, it is Seneca's pupil Nero who is remembered for his excessive cruelty in this area, including his introduction of the practice of throwing Christians to the lions.

executions of criminals were not considered worthy of comment, so we have little idea of the early ways of staging the public executions.

Under the Republic it would appear that Roman citizens were exempt from the death penalty. If they committed especially serious crimes they found themselves banished from Rome or, in extreme cases, from all Roman territory. For a citizen of Rome this could be serious punishment indeed. Not only was the person separated from friends, family and wealth, but was made vulnerable prey to any brigands or crooks who chose to take advantage of the exile.

An exception came in times of war when those who turned traitor or abandoned their duty could be executed. This rule dated back to the very earliest days of Rome when the Capitoline Hill was under siege from the Samnites in 750 BC. Tarpeia, daughter of the heroic Spurius Tarpeius, promised to open the gates in return for a large collection of jewellery.

Tarpeia died for her treachery and it became traditional for later traitors to be hurled to their deaths down the sheer sides of the Capitoline Hill at a spot called the Tarpeian Rock. As the Empire expanded, it was not always convenient to carry a malefactor back to the Tarpeian Rock, so beheading became standard practice.

As time passed the concept of treason became somewhat flexible. In the later Republic executions could be ordered for defrauding the state of tax money as well as for aiding an enemy. Under the Emperors, treason became an even wider crime category as it grew to cover disagreeing with the Emperor or simply annoying him in some way. But then public executions of citizens gradually became less common occurrences. Citizens condemned to death were often granted a day or two in which to set their affairs in order. This gave them the chance to commit suicide and to die surrounded by their family and friends rather than by a baying mob.

For non-citizens living in Rome the law was harsher. Punishments tended to be swift and immediate, taking the forms of beatings, floggings and amputations as well as the criminal's being condemned to work as a labourer in state mines or on building projects. The death penalty was imposed for a wider range of crimes than was applicable for a citizen. Murder was punishable in a non-citizen by death but by exile if the killer was a citizen.

Such niceties were not always observed. In the sixties AD the Governor of Spain, Servius Galba, ordered the execution by crucifixion of a man who had murdered his nephew in order to gain the family inheritance. The condemned man protested against the punishment not because he was innocent but because his status as a citizen forbade the death penalty for murder. Governor Galba nodded sagely then ordered guards 'Make this man's cross higher than usual to show his status.' Galba went on to order a dishonest money changer to have both hands chopped off and nailed to the door of the his business.

Such actions were justified by Roman lawyers who held that punishment should have one of three aims. Either it should reform the person being punished, or it should deter others from committing similar crimes, or it should make society safer by removing a criminal from circulation. In pursuing these Roman concepts of justice and punishment the small print of the law was sometimes ignored. That the Romans generally supported such an attitude is shown by the fact that in AD 68 Governor Galba was invited to become Emperor by the Senate in the hope that he could sort out the corruption and dishonesty that had become endemic in government service under Nero.

Slaves, being mere property, could expect none of the legal safeguards that even a non-citizen received. Trials for slaves were unheard of at any period. It was entirely up to the owner of a slave to determine his guilt or innocence of any alleged crime, and to decide on a suitable punishment.

Not all owners made sensible choices when it came to punishing slaves. During the rule of Nero a man named Glyco discovered his wife in bed with one of his slaves. The outraged Glyco at once ordered the public execution of the slave. The move merely served to publicize the fact that his wife preferred a slave to himself and made him the butt of numerous ribald and obscene jokes.

Perhaps with this example in mind, Hadrian made it illegal for a man to condemn his slave to death on his own authority. If a man felt a slave deserved to be executed, he had to take the case to a magistrate who alone had the right to order the death penalty. The same statute forbade female slaves being forced into prostitution or male slaves turned into gladiators without the magistrates' approval.

The determination of the Romans to ensure that the punishment of criminals should deter others from being tempted to follow a life of crime was what drove the more bizarre and cruel punishments of the arena. Public humiliation was thought essential and the worse the crime the greater the loss of dignity and pride that the criminal should expect before death finally claimed him. This, naturally, meant that punishments had to take place in public.

At first the Forum was considered a suitable venue for executions, which took place soon after the trial of the criminal. By the early first century BC, however, citizens staging a *munus* or gladiatorial games were being given the task of carrying out the executions. The development spared the state the bother of imprisoning or executing criminals, while those staging spectacles gained a valuable new attraction to their games. This was especially the case if the person to be dispatched was a notorious bandit or had committed a much publicized crime. The editor, or person staging the games, bore the full costs.

At first the executions were included in the programme of events almost at random. Later, however, it became customary to hold the executions at lunchtime. The respectable senators, knights and rich citizens left their reserved seats to dine or rest as the hottest part of the day passed. The plebeians who had queued for the best views risked losing their places if they left to get something to eat, so they tended to stay at the ringside. Editors soon realized that they needed to provide something for the plebs to watch, but were reluctant to put trained gladiators or expensive animals into the arena when the influential nobility were not present. The executions were the answer. How the spectators managed to eat their lunches when the horrors were taking place is difficult to imagine.

These condemned men and women were known as the noxii. Unlike gladiators or *venatores*, the noxii had no hope of survival at a games. Their task was to die for the benefit of society and the enjoyment of the crowd. The ways in which they died were terrible indeed.

Some executions were relatively straightforward. The condemned man might be beheaded or stabbed. However such simple deaths provided little in the way of entertainment for the mob. So a more lively variant was to give one of the noxii a weapon and instruct him to kill all the others. Only when this gory duty was done was the killer himself killed. More entertaining for the mob was the procession of death described by the poet Seneca in the first century AD. A pair of criminals was pushed into the arena, one of whom had a knife or other simple weapon. He killed his opponent, then was forcibly disarmed by the guards. A new prisoner was brought in and given the knife to despatch the man who had just done the killing. One after another the prisoners were brought in to kill the ones before them until all were dead.

Sometimes the noxii might be dressed in gladiatorial armour and sent into the arena to face highly-trained gladiators. These were treated as exhibition bouts in which the veteran fighters would show off their best moves and techniques against the hapless amateur before moving in to administer a quick death for the adoring crowd.

Perhaps the best-known fate of the noxii was to be thrown to the lions, a fate which popular imagination has as the usual punishment for Christians. As so often in the world of the Roman arena, things were not that simple.

The idea of throwing humans to wild animals as a form of death sentence came from Carthage. This enormously powerful city in North Africa ruled a large empire and monopolized vast and hugely profitable trading routes across the western Mediterranean. The city fought three long wars with Rome between 264 and 146 BC which ended with the total destruction of Carthage. During these conflicts, Carthage not only used her own troops but also hired large numbers of mercenaries. These men were paid generous wages, but also subjected to harsh punishments. Any Carthaginian or mercenary who defected to Rome was executed by being thrown into a pit containing hungry lions.

The Romans adopted this method of execution as punishment for the most disgraceful of crimes and elaborated it. A noxii condemned to be killed by beasts or *damnati ad bestias*, was held in prison until the day came for his or her execution. Then the unfortunate was moved near to the arena where the games were taking place and securely chained. When the time for execution came, the criminal was led into the arena, preceded by a man carrying a placard on which was clearly written the name and crime of the condemned. If the criminal was especially notorious he might be led around the edge of the arena so that the crowd could get a good look.

The criminal was then taken to the centre of the arena and tied to a post, the placard being fixed over his head. These posts, or *stipes*, were made in a variety of shapes. Some were simply upright stakes. Others were a horizontal bar between two uprights from which the condemned dangled by their arms or legs. One mosaic shows condemned men tied to chariots, though without horses.

Once the condemned person, or persons, were tied securely in place the beasts were released. Lions were used for this purpose, as were tigers and leopards. They were usually starved for some days before an execution to ensure that they would attack with promptness and savagery. Ferocious as these beasts were, they did at least kill with a single bite or blow of the paw, thus giving the hapless criminal a speedy death. Other beasts used to despatch noxii were not so swift in dealing out death. Crocodiles, wolves, dogs and bears were all used on occasion. Death at the hands of these beasts was a slow and painful affair. Sometimes a human was sent in to finish off the victim, not through any sense of mercy but to get the killing over with in time to move on to the next event.

It was to this degrading and painful death that the Romans, in popular imagination, sent the Christians by the thousands. It is difficult to be precise about how many Christians were actually executed and how many of those were flung to the lions or other beasts. Records either have not survived or are unreliable.

We do know, however, that the first persecution of the Christians took place under the Emperor Nero in the summer of AD 64. In the course of the long, hot summer, Rome caught fire and burned for nine days. Much of the central part of the city was utterly destroyed. Nero set about clearing the ruins for redevelopment, seized the prime site for himself and began building a magnificent new palace. Soon rumours spread that he had begun the fire deliberately to clear the ground. To quash these rumours, Nero began his own rumours that the fire had been started by the Christians, then a small and secretive sect which had most of its support among slaves or the poor. Nero ordered the arrest of any Christians who could be identified and condemned them to death. Some were thrown to the wild beasts of the arena, others were crucified. Traditionally St Peter the apostle died in this persecution.

Nero's persecution was spasmodic and opportunistic, but later assaults on the Christian community were more determined and methodical. The Romans were famously tolerant of religious differences and welcomed many foreign gods into Rome. The difficulty they encountered in dealing with the Christians was that they claimed their God was the only God, and stated quite openly that all other gods were devils or imaginary. More seriously, the Christians refused to perform sacrifices to what they viewed as fake gods. This meant the Christians would not take part in the rituals which bound the Roman citizenry together and which upheld the Roman state. In the practical politics of the day this refusal made them traitors.

In the year 177 the city of Lugdunum, now Lyons, saw a major persecution of the Christians. In that year Easter happened to fall on the same day as the festival of hilaria, sacred to the goddess Cybele. Both festivals involved both secret and public rites and there seems to have been some conflict between rival processions. The priests of Cybele promptly denounced the Christians as traitors to Rome on the grounds that they refused to carry out the state rites. The Christians were arrested and given the chance to perform the state sacrifices, but refused. They were then sent to the arena to be killed by beasts. In this instance the data has survived to show that forty-eight leading Christians were killed. Bad as this figure is, it is surprisingly low for such a major and well known persecution.

The later Great Persecution under the Emperor Diocletian began in 297 and lasted for over five years. Contemporary Christian writers recorded mass executions, with torture and humiliation commonplace. The persecution began with the removal from government posts of any who would not carry out the traditional rituals. The arrest of Christian clergy followed in 303 and in 304 began the execution of the more recalcitrant Christians. More distress was caused because as well as the executions the state found it convenient to confiscate the lands and wealth of the Christian Church.

Just as Nero began the habit of throwing Christians to lions, so he also began another truly horrific practice. Nero believed himself to be a great poet, singer and dramatist and would frequently stage his own works for the delight of his guests or for the populace as a whole. In AD 62 Nero travelled to Greece to take part in the great literary and artistic festivals of the Greek world. He competed against the best playwrights, singers and actors and was delighted, though perhaps not surprised, when the judges tactfully awarded first prize in every event to the emperor. The tour of Greece reinforced in Nero's mind not just the reality of his artistic gifts, which were in reality good but not outstanding, but also a devotion to Greek culture.

On his return to Rome, Nero wrote an epic poem about the fall of Troy which was intended for public recitation. Nero then moved on to a work about the great hero Heracles, known in Rome as Hercules. It was at this point that an unfortunate thief by the name of Meniscus was apprehended while stealing apples from Nero's garden. Theft of the Emperor's property was judged to be treason and the hapless Meniscus was condemned to death. Hearing of this, Nero had an idea.

The result was that Meniscus was made the unwilling star performer of Nero's drama about Hercules. He appeared only in the final scene, taking the place of the actor who had previously played the hero. In myth, Heracles dies when his wife Deianeira gives him a coat smeared with the blood of the centaur Nessus. This magical blood reacts against the semi-divine flesh of Heracles and bursts into flame, consuming the hero in an agonising fire. Meniscus was clothed in a coat smeared in pitch, set alight and pushed on to the stage. His searing death agonies forming the triumphal end to Nero's play.

Unfortunately for the noxii, the idea of staging their executions in the form of dramatic performances proved popular. Some legends were staged time and again. The story of Orpheus soothing the savage beast with the beauty of his music was a favourite subject. The condemned man would be given a lyre to play and pushed into an arena filled with harmless goats, deer or sheep. To win his life, the man was told, he had to charm the animals with music for a set period of time, or reach the far side of the arena. More often than not a ferocious lion, bear or other beast was released at some point in the performance and the man torn to pieces.

Almost as popular for reenactment was the legend of Dirce. This terrifying legendary Queen of Thebes was unwise enough to pick on her more attractive niece Antiope who was loved by the great god Zeus, by whom the girl had twin sons. These sons later avenged their mother's years of pain and humiliation by tying Dirce to a bull, which gored her to death. Women condemned to death could find themselves tied to a bull in a variety of ways as the final act in plays retelling the legend of Dirce. In one bizarre version, the unfortunate was strapped to the bull's back as the bull was attacked by a pride of lions.

Other mythical tales were less easy to recreate or required elaborate stage machinery and so were not staged so often. One of these was the legend of Daedalus and Icarus. In Greek legend the Athenian master craftsman Daedalus and his equally gifted son Icarus were held prisoner by King Minos of Crete who forced them to complete statues and buildings without payment. Daedalus hatched a plan to escape their mountaintop prison by building artificial wings out of bird feathers attached to a framework by wax. The wings worked perfectly, and the two men launched themselves into the air to fly over the Aegean Sea to home. The youthful Icarus, however, got carried away and flew too close to the sun, which melted the wax on his wings. The feathers came off and he plunged to his death.

In the gory version staged in the arena, two noxii would have feathered wings strapped to their backs and be launched over the heads of the crowds on ropes. The mechanism was rigged so that when the pair reached a point over the centre of the arena, the ropes broke and they fell to their deaths on the sand far below. Beasts might then be released to finish off the injured criminals.

Pseudo-historic recreations were also staged. Soon after a notorious Sicilian bandit named Selurus was killed on the slopes of Mount Etna, the event was restaged in the Roman arena. To add variety to the performance, the artificial mountain was built of wood and had concealed within it cages, holding animals, which were rigged to open if the noxii playing Selurus and his gang stepped on hidden catches. It was a bear which finally got the man playing Selurus and tore him to pieces.

It was no wonder that some prisoners preferred suicide to an appearance in the arena. One captive from a rebellious German tribe was due to appear in one such performance and was under close guard. He persuaded the guards to let him go to the toilet alone. Once in the toilet he picked up the stick with a sponge on the end that was provided in all public toilets for bottom cleaning and rammed it down his throat so that he choked to death. 'Not a very elegant way to die,' commented the philosopher Seneca who recorded the incident, 'but there is no point being fussy about our departure. He was a brave man.' No doubt many others wished they had been able to follow the example of the nameless German rather than enter the arena as a noxii.

The techniques the Romans developed for disposing of the criminals they had condemned to death were both terrifying and ingenious. Still more ingenious and impressive were the buildings in which these dreadful events took place. Amphitheatres were purpose built for the games of blood in many cities across the Empire. But the greatest of them all stood in Rome: the Colosseum.

IX

ᐧ THE COLOSSEUM ᐧ

I N THE POPULAR IMAGINATION gladiatorial games took place in purpose built arenas in front of baying mobs of thousands of Romans. In fact, the earliest gladiatorial contests took place either beside the tomb of the man being honoured by a *munus* or on his estate. There would have been few spectators other than the dead man's family and household.

Later, as the events became spectacles and attracted large crowds, they were held in town squares or, in Rome, at the Forum. In these venues the editor of the games, the man putting on the spectacle, might erect temporary wooden seating for the comfort of the audience. The erection of permanent structures in which games could be held did not begin until the first century BC. Only then were the events being staged frequently enough for the large expense of permanent buildings to be worthwhile.

The oldest gladiatorial amphitheatre of which enough remains for us to see the layout in any detail is that in Pompeii. The structure was built in 80 BC and had seating capacity of about 20,000. We know of earlier amphitheatres from written sources, but these were built at least partially of wood and so have not survived. The Pompeii amphitheatre is built entirely of stone and includes several features that were to become standard elements of amphitheatre design across the Roman Empire.

The most consistent feature of all amphitheatres was their shape, an elliptical oval. The most effective layout to give all spectators a good view of the action in the arena would have been a circle, but that would have

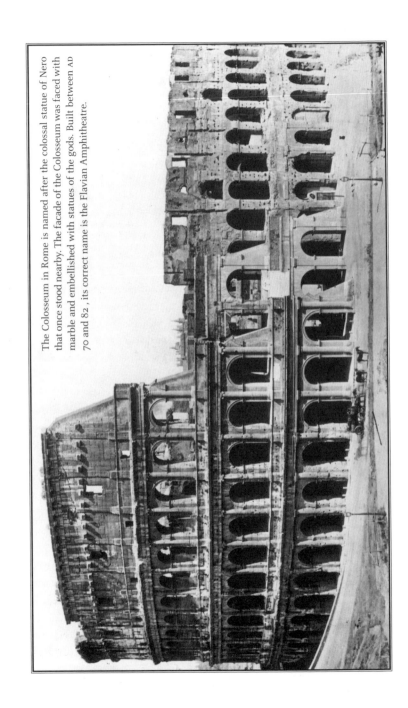

The Colosseum in Rome is named after the colossal statue of Nero that once stood nearby. The facade of the Colosseum was faced with marble and embellished with statues of the gods. Built between AD 70 and 82, its correct name is the Flavian Amphitheatre.

been of little use for the primary purpose of the games by this date which was to enhance the prestige and fame of the editor of the games, and thus his chances of winning elections. The elliptical oval, however, gave a position of prominence for the special dais on which sat the editor. This dais was placed half way along the shady, northern side where the curve was at its flattest. From there the editor could see everything that went on in the arena or in the seating. More importantly, he could be seen by the entire crowd. The platform on which he sat went by the name of the tribunal editoris. The arena itself was covered with sand to soak up the blood and give the fighters a good grip with their feet. The word arena comes from the Latin for sand.

A second feature of the amphitheatre at Pompeii that was to persist was the location of the two gates which gave access to the arena itself. These were put in at either end of the oval. One was dubbed the Porta Libitinaria, named after Libitina the goddess of burials. It was through this gate that the dead, be they human or animal, were removed for disposal.

A third characteristic set by the Pompeii amphitheatre was the layout of the seating. The seats were made of stone and ran in horizontal lines around the arena. The front seats were raised several feet above the sand and separated from it by a sheer wall of polished stone. This was a safety feature as the wall stopped beasts or frantic men from climbing into the crowd. Sometimes nets were rigged above the wall for added safety. The long horizontal rows of seats were broken by vertical flights of steps so that each block of seats formed a wedge-shape. At the top of the steps was a door through which the crowd entered and left the amphitheatre.

Finally, the amphitheatre of Pompeii was built by two extremely wealthy local magnates named Gaius Quintius Valgus and March Porcius. These men made sure that a prominent inscription recorded their generosity for posterity, and for the attention of the voting public. The fashion was followed elsewhere and with other public buildings. The construction of an amphitheatre was as much a method of gaining public approval as building a temple.

In one important respect the Pompeii amphitheatre is unique. It was built by digging down into the ground so that the floor of the arena was some feet below the level of the ground. The soil excavated was heaped up to form the banks on which the stone seats were built. This model was not followed elsewhere. Most amphitheatres were entirely free standing structures whether they were built of wood, stone or a mix of the two.

In Rome itself the first permanent amphitheatre was built in 29 BC, but this part wood and part stone construction was destroyed by the great fire of AD 64. Eight years later the newly-installed Emperor Vespasian began the construction of a replacement. His amphitheatre was to become the largest and most impressive of the entire Roman world: the Colosseum.

As with so much related to the spectacles and free entertainments of Rome, the building of the Colosseum was all about pleasing the voting mob and holding on to power. The new emperor, Titus Flavius Vespasianus, was a career army officer from the Sabine country. His family, the Flavians, were provincial landowners rather than an old aristocratic Roman family. When Nero committed suicide, power had been seized by Galba, who held office for less than a year before he was murdered by the Praetorian Guard, led by one of Nero's supporters who then became Emperor Otho. Four months later Otho faced the rebellious legions of the Rhine frontier who had declared their own commander, Vitellius as emperor. Otho lost the Battle of Cremona and committed suicide. Vitellius became Rome's third emperor in less than a year.

Within four months the armies stationed in the east and along the Danube declared that Vespasian was their choice for emperor and marched on Rome. Vespasian's elder brother was in Rome at the time and fled to the ancient Temple of Jupiter on the Capitoline Hill for safety. Vitellius had the sacred temple burned to the ground and most of the buildings on the Capitol were destroyed as well. In December AD 69 Vespasian's troops arrived at Rome, fought their way into the city and butchered Vitellius.

Vespasian was faced with the task of restoring the morale of Rome after eighteen months of turmoil and bloodshed. He not only had to reimpose the bureaucracy and government of the Empire, but quite literally had to rebuild much of the city of Rome. He decided to combine the two tasks and launched an ambitious construction programme.

The first building to go up was a new Temple of Jupiter on the Capitol. Vespasian built in the Greek style and on a large scale, the finished temple being not much smaller than the Parthenon in Athens. This lavish project associated Vespasian with the values of old Rome and with the culture of Greece. Next was the Temple of the Deified Claudius, work on which had been abandoned by Nero and his successors. Finishing work on this temple linked Vespasian to the popular family of Julius Caesar, but subtly distanced him from the incompetent regimes of Nero, Galba, Otho and Vitellius.

Finally, Vespasian turned to pleasing the mob of Roman plebeians. The new emperor knew that it was on his popularity with the voting public that the continuation of his rule would ultimately depend. By gaining control of the means of patronage as firmly as had Augustus, Vespasian could establish a secure regime and pass power on to his sons, Titus and Domitian. And nothing pleased the plebeians so much as the games.

Since the fire of AD 64 Rome had been without a purpose-built amphitheatre. Vespasian summoned the finest masons and builders to design for Rome the most magnificent stadium incorporating all the latest high-tech features of the arena. It was a naked bid for support from the lower orders of Roman society and it worked brilliantly. Not only did Vespasian succeed in holding on to power until his death in AD 79, but power then passed smoothly first to his eldest son Titus then to the younger son Domitian.

Vespasian chose the site for his amphitheatre well. It lay at one end of the Forum Romanum, nestled between the Palatine and Esquiline Hills. It was therefore located on the edge of the commercial and religious centre of Rome and yet close to the densely packed residential districts. Perhaps more importantly it was on the site of pleasure gardens created by Nero for his palace which in its turn had been built on the site of houses destroyed in the fire of AD 64. Again, Vespasian was making a clear statement that he was making a break with Nero. Where Nero had taken parts of Rome for his private pleasure, Vespasian was returning them to the people of Rome.

Building work began in AD 74 and lasted for years. The project included not only the amphitheatre itself, but also the surrounding area. The land around the new building was levelled off and paved with slabs of lava. In this open space was left upright one of the few survivals from Nero's pleasure grounds, an enormous statue of himself made of gilded bronze. Standing 120 feet high this statue was simply too impressive to be swept away. Instead, Vespasian removed the inscriptions from the base identifying it as Nero, added some metal spikes to the head that looked a bit like sun rays and rededicated the statue as a sun god.

In the midst of this imposing open space slowly rose the great Flavian Amphitheatre, although it did not acquire its modern name until some centuries after the last Games were held there. The area of the structure was huge, much larger than that of any other amphitheatre, being 620 feet by 510 feet. The exterior face was massively grand, rising to 157 feet in height. The facade was divided into four storeys, though there were five within it.

The ground floor was made up of eighty arches, each of which was a numbered spectator entrance, separated by robust doric columns. The second storey was similar in that it had another eighty arches, though each of these served as a frame for a graceful statue, and the pillars were of the more delicate ionic style. The third storey had smaller arches and statues and columns of the flamboyantly graceful corinthian style. Above this was a blank facade broken up by corinthian pilasters and square windows. The top of the facade was lined by a row of bronze shields and topped by stone posts.

This, at least, was the facade as it was completed by Titus in AD 80. The Emperor held a magnificent series of games lasting 100 days in the arena to celebrate its completion. Again there was a political motive for Titus was newly in power and wished to ingratiate himself with the masses. The Flavian Amphitheatre would be changed and updated many times over the years, especially after AD 217 when a bolt of lightning struck the building and caused massive damage that took more than twelve years to repair.

Within the Colosseum, the builders introduced a number of novel features. The first was the installation of a second tribunal editoris facing the first. Called the *pulvinar*, this was a form of royal box for the Emperor and his personal guests to occupy. It faced the seat reserved for the editor of the games. It was normal practice for the Emperor to stage the games, but to do so to honour a successful general or close family member. The Emperor would sit on the pulvinar, the person being honoured on the tribunal editoris.

The seating in the Colosseum was, at first, varied for each event or series of games. It was up to the Emperor to decide who got reserved seats and who had to join the queue to occupy the free seats. No doubt the distribution of the best seats was used as yet another part of the system of clientage and patronage that dominated Roman society and government. Later the arrangements became more formalized. The seating closest to the arena was reserved for senators, their male relatives and prominent knights, though one small section was set aside for the Vestal Virgins.

Behind the seats for the Senators sat the citizens of Rome who did not aspire to great wealth or to aristocratic ancestry. This section comprised the main bulk of the audience. The seats were numbered and carefully allocated, though quite how remains unclear. The entrances on the outside of the ground floor were numbered, as were the seating rows, and tokens have been found in Rome which correlate to these. Presumably the clay tokens were handed out to citizens in the run up to the staging of a *munus*.

Above and behind the open banks of seating were a number of covered arcades and areas of flat standing room. These were where women, foreigners and slaves stood to watch the events in the arena. Although they were some distance away from the scene of action, these standing areas still had a good view and the Colosseum's skilful acoustics meant that every grunt, snarl or scream could be clearly heard.

The capacity of the Colosseum is a matter of some debate. Ancient writers record that during especially impressive events over 70,000 people packed into the amphitheatre. Modern estimates based on the size of the Colosseum and comparing that with modern football stadiums puts the capacity at a more modest 45,000 people. Perhaps the Romans were not too fussy about comfort and would squeeze into any available space.

In building this massive structure, the Roman engineers used every architectural trick they knew. The lower parts were built with massive pillars and arches constructed of travertine, a white limestone from Tivoli. These could support the weight of the building above but still looked ornamental. The middle storeys were made of concrete, then a relatively new building material, which was lighter and could be poured into moulds, making possible the intricate network of passageways used by the citizens on their way to their seats. The uppermost sections were built of brick and volcanic stone, both of which were relatively light but still able to support the crowds that thronged the upper storeys. The exterior was faced with travertine at all levels to create an impressive facade.

At the very top of the banked rows of seats and standing spaces was the forest of stone posts and wooden poles that supported the ingenious Colosseum roof. This *velarium* was a gigantic sunshade made of canvas or leather and supported by ropes and wooden poles. Exactly how the velarium was operated is unclear. It was worked by teams of sailors drafted in from the fleet and who were presumably adept at handling sails, which worked on a similar system of canvas and ropes. It is likely that the shade could be pulled across most of the open space for there are accounts of the air getting stuffy in the afternoon. Water could be sprayed on the audience if the temperature rose too high. The poor performers in the arena, of course, had no such luxuries.

The floor of the arena changed greatly during the active life of the Colosseum. When it was first built the floor was solid earth, covered over with sand. The site had been partly occupied by an ornamental lake in the days of Nero's gardens and Vespasian retained the piping that had fed and drained the lake. In the early years of the Colosseum's life the arena was sometimes flooded either for displays involving crocodiles, seals, dolphins or other water-based animals or for naval battles fought between small scale warships with just a few rowers each.

During the second century AD, the water pipes were removed and the area under the arena floor was excavated to provide a maze of subterranean rooms and corridors. These were used to house a wide variety of sophisticated stage machinery. There were lifts, trapdoors and chutes from which gladiators or wild beasts could suddenly appear. There were moving sections of floor which could be pulled aside so that an entire section of scenery, such as a forest or fortress, could rise up from underground to delight the audience.

It is these underground chambers that show most clearly that the Colosseum and other amphitheatres like it, were merely the public face of an entire industry dedicated to serving the bloody drama of the Games.

X

⁌ THEATRES OF BLOOD ⁌

B Y THE FIRST CENTURY AD, the format of a *munus*, or show in the amphitheatre, had become well established. The crowd knew what it was likely to see, although novelties were always welcome, and the editor staging the show knew what he had to provide.

Some weeks before the event was due to take place the editor, who was holding the munus to honour a dead father, uncle or other relative, would contact the *lanista* of his local gladiatorial troupe, or would choose one out of several if he was in an area with more than one lanista running a business. Together the two men would decide how elaborate the munus was to be, how many gladiators would perform, how many animals would be displayed and a whole list of other details. Much depended on how much hard cash the editor was willing to pay, and to what extent he could bargain prices down with the lanista. Once agreement had been reached, the editor had relatively little to do except turn up on the day and enjoy the adulation of the crowd.

It was the lanista who would send out men skilled in sign writing to daub graffiti on the public walls. These notices detailed the date and time of the munus, where it was to take place and who was the editor. As the date approached, the signs would be rewritten to boast of the programme of events and the lavishness of the coming display. Two or three days before the munus there was usually a parade through the streets or the Forum. The gladiators would march in column, closely followed by boys

This photograph of the interior of the Colosseum reveals the elaborate network of passages, wild animal pens and cells that were concealed by the sand floor of the arena.

carrying their weapons. The wild beasts were trundled along in cages on carts and the various performers would follow behind. The night before the games it was traditional for the gladiators, animal hunters and others to be treated to a sumptuous banquet by the editor of the munus. This *cena libera*, as it was known, always took place in a public area so that the crowd could come to eye up the combatants who would be in the next day's events.

The day of the munus began early as those without reserved places queued up to get good seats in the public areas. Later, those honoured guests, usually men to whom the editor owed a favour or from whom he wanted one, would arrive and take their numbered seats near the front.

Finally the show began with a grand procession into the arena. First came civic dignitaries or magistrates who symbolized the power of the state and reminded everyone present that no matter how popular or powerful the editor might be, it was the state and the emperor that really counted. These men were followed by trumpeters, whose braying instruments alerted the crowd to the arrival of the gladiators who followed. Again, servants carried the arms and armour of the fighters. Next came a litter carried on the shoulders of priests which supported cult statues of the town's patron gods as well as Mars, Victory, Nemesis and other gods suitable to the bloodthirsty games about to commence. More musicians followed, after which came the animal hunters, acrobats and other performers. Among these were the grim figures of men dressed as the god Mercury and Charon, the ferryman who carried the souls of the dead to Hades. These men had the task of disposing of the dead bodies of men and beasts. Mercury carried a rod with which to poke the bodies before Charon moved in. Partly this was to show the crowd that death was real, but also to reassure the man dressed as Charon. He would not want an apparently lifeless lion suddenly to wake up while being wheeled out of the arena.

Finally the editor of the munus arrived riding in a beautifully ornate four-horse chariot and dressed in a toga of the finest woollen cloth, embroidered with gold and purple. He was adorned with the best jewellery money could buy and carried in his hand a white silk handkerchief, again richly embroidered, with which he would give his signals to the lanista as the munus progressed. All this finery was, usually, hired from the lanista. There might follow a short speech outlining the merits of the man being honoured, then the procession exited and the editor took his seat.

First to perform were the musicians, who were placed at one end of the arena in the front of the seating area. Most instruments were varieties of trumpet and horn, but the water organ was also played. This peculiar instrument was invented by a Greek named Ctesibius in Alexandria about 240 BC. The key to the operation of the water organ, or *hydraulis*, was pressurized air. One or two assistants used bellows to pump air into an inverted metal bowl set in a large barrel of water. As the air was pumped in it was compressed by the weight of water it displaced. A network of tubes led from the air bowl to a series of organ pipes. When the musician pressed a key it opened the tube to a pipe, allowing a stream of high-pressure air to rush through. Water organs were much louder than their hand operated counterparts and, with the air flow evened out by the water pressure, more likely to be played in tune.

Once everyone was ready, the first act in the munus could begin. This was usually the *venationes*, the wild animal show. Some animals were hunted down by humans, others set to fight each other in supposed recreation of the wild world that Rome had tamed. Still others were brought on to perform tricks. Next came the amusing clowns and acrobats with parodies of topical events and feats of physical dexterity.

As the light hearted displays were drawing to a close, the seats of those privileged to have reserved places began to empty. The editor of the games would have provided a sumptuous lunch for these honoured guests in a nearby room. While the editor and his guests dined, the mob in the free seats stayed sitting down jealously guarding the places they had queued for. To keep these people amused while the important folk dined, condemned criminals were led into the arena to be butchered in a variety of ingenious ways.

After the executions, slaves came out with fresh sand to scatter over the blood and gore before the gladiators arrived. First came a piece of business. The editor, lanista and some attendants entered the arena for the *pompa* ceremony. First the attendants produced the gladiatorial weapons. The editor used these to slice open a variety of fruits and vegetables to show that they were sufficiently sharp for their gruesome purpose. Next the names of the gladiators to fight that afternoon were written on wooden tablets and placed in a large bowl. The editor then pulled out the names to decide who would face whom. This was a complicated business as the correct type of gladiator had to be matched against a suitable opponent. Nobody wanted to see a *retiarius* fight another retiarius if there was a *secutor* available. The results of the draw were then announced to the crowd.

Then the real fighting would begin as the first pair of gladiators took to the arena. Usually the gladiators fought pair after pair, so that the crowd could concentrate its attention on the skill of one set of combatants at a time. This pair by pair fighting also ensured that the gladiators paid for by the editor lasted as long as possible. Only the most wealthy editor would put more than two gladiators into the arena at once, and even then they would be the least experienced and cheapest. As each combat ended, whether in death or in *missus*, the victor approached the editor for his palm of victory and his prize money.

At the end of the day, after the final gladiatorial fight had reached its bloody conclusion, came the *sparsio*. The editor of the games, in a final burst of generosity, had gifts thrown into the crowd. Sometimes these were handfuls of coins hurled by burly slaves, but on other occasions the editors were more imaginative. Then they had numbered tokens thrown into the crowd instead of money. The tokens were later redeemed for a prize from the editor's house or business. This gave the editor an opportunity to impress on the lucky winners that they had him to thank, and allowed him to drop pointed hints about when the next elections were due. These prizes for tokens traditionally varied wildly in value. One might be a basket of fruit, another an embroidered cloak and a third a new house.

By the year AD 100 the *munera* had become vast shows. They therefore required not only a purpose built amphitheatre, but also a whole range of support industries that kept thousands of people in jobs, albeit some of them as slaves.

It is relatively obvious and straightforward what some of the backup industries needed to be. There were the armourers who made and maintained the weapons and armour of the gladiators and *venatores*. Equally necessary were the seamstresses who made the festive clothing for the editor and his family and the carpenters who produced the chariots and other stage props used during the munera.

But there were other, less obvious tasks that needed to be done. Gladiator helmets were adorned with showy feathers to add to the spectacle and extravagance of the munera. So farms were needed where peacocks and pheasants could be reared, cared for and have their feathers plucked. The constant demand for fresh sand in the arena meant that gangs of workmen were employed to dig sand from the nearest beach or sandy area, load it on to carts and shift it to storage bins outside the arena.

And the wild animals had to be kept somewhere before their appearances in the shows. With hundreds of beasts being killed in a single munus, the need for cages could be immense. The menageries of Rome became something of an attraction for visitors and idlers in their own right. We know that during the reign of Augustus a total of 400 tigers, 250 lions and 600 leopards passed through the menagerie reserved for the big cats. Some of these beasts were slaughtered in the arena, but others were kept for the despatch of criminals and a few were trained in the same manner as modern circus animals. There are no records of the numbers of bears, deer, boars, wolves, seals, elephants and the vast array of other animals that we know were kept for the great games in the capital city, but the numbers must have been equally huge. The menageries needed animal keepers to look after the beasts in their cages. They needed farms to raise grass and leaves to feed the herbivores and sheep or goats to feed the carnivores. And they needed teams of carters to haul the food from the farms to the menageries. All this required workmen, and these men had to be housed and fed. Keeping the menageries was no easy task.

Nor was filling the menageries with animals at all straightforward. The Roman mob demanded exotic animals of terrifying ferocity to appear before them. There was no excitement in seeing an Italian deer being slaughtered, but an Arabian oryx was something else. Right across the Empire there stretched a network of hunters, markets and transports which employed thousands of men on the sole task of bringing animals to Rome to die in the amphitheatre.

In some areas the provincial governor employed teams of professional hunters to go out and capture whatever was required by Rome. In

Germany the Legion I Minervia had one cohort which was exempt from duty patrolling the turbulent German tribes and spent all its time catching wolves and bears. But local herdsmen and hunters were continually on the lookout for the chance to capture a creature that would earn them a good sum of money. Over the years various techniques of capturing the desired animals were perfected.

In North Africa, leopards were caught by digging a deep pit and building around it a short wall just high enough to stop a passing leopard seeing the pit behind. A goat was then put in the pit. Hearing the helpless prey and sensing an easy meal, the leopard would leap over the wall and fall into the pit from which it could not escape. A baited cage was lowered into the pit. The big cat was then lured inside and the cage hauled up to be placed on a cart.

In the Middle East, lions were taken as cubs. If the enraged mother intervened, one cub would be dropped so that while the lioness gently carried her youngster back to the den, the hunters could escape with the others. Around the Black Sea a more ingenious method for taking adult lions was used. Trackers would locate a stream or pool where a lion was accustomed to drink. A trough of water heavily laced with wine was placed by the stream or pool. When the lion drank and became inebriated it would be bundled into a cage for transport.

In Numidia, south of Egypt, high fences many miles in length were constructed across an area of bush. The fences slowly converged to form a funnel, ending in a large enclosure. Beaters were then strung out over a vast area of land and moved forward, driving ostriches, zebra, antelope and apes before them until they became trapped in the enclosure. Then men with lassoes moved in to extract whichever animals were needed and dragged them into cages.

The larger beasts, such as elephants and rhinoceroses, caused all sorts of problems in transportation because of their sheer bulk and power. The containers had to be made of thick balks of timber and dozens of men had to strain on the ropes lifting them from cart to ship and back again. Nor were elephants easy to catch. The Romans soon learned that there was little point luring an elephant into a pit as the others in the herd would stomp the edges of the pit until they collapsed and the prisoner could escape. Instead these beasts had to be lured into stoutly built stockades. This might seem a tricky task, but the ancient hunters mastered it to such an extent that by AD 350 the diminutive North African species of elephant was extinct. Also driven to extinction by the constant demand for arena animals was the Balkan lion, the cheetah of the Middle East and an unknown number of subspecies and varieties of other animals. The activities in the arena had an impact far beyond Rome.

The scale of the killing in the arena was prodigious, and it lasted for centuries. Some 700 years passed between the first munus and the last, but the games were so popular that the mere wiping out of certain species of animal was not enough to make anyone think they should be stopped. The great spectacles were going to need something more dramatic than a loss of Balkan lions to close them down.

XI

، THE END OF THE ،
GLADIATORS

I N AD 350 THE GLADIATORIAL GAMES were as popular, magnificent and widespread as they had ever been. An unbroken history
of development and adaptation stretching back some 600 years lay
behind the combats. A century later not a single gladiator, *lanista* or
munus was to be found anywhere.

For an institution that had survived for so long and been so popular
to disappear so completely was dramatic indeed. Some have claimed it
was Christianity that abolished the gladiators, some that it was the fall of
Rome. But the end of the gladiators was rather more complex than either
idea would suggest.

Although Christian writers denounced the gladiatorial games, they
were not the first to voice criticism. The first century AD philosopher
Lucius Annaeus Seneca came to Rome to work as a lawyer, later becoming tutor to the young Nero and in time his chief minister. Seneca had no
time for the gladiatorial games. He wrote that 'Man is a thing which is
sacred to humanity, but nowadays he is killed in play or for fun. It was
once a sin to teach how to inflict wounds, but now a man is led out naked
and defenceless and provides a good show by his death.' He also criti-
cized those who attended such events saying that those who watch the
killings 'come home more greedy, more ambitious, more voluptuous,
more cruel and inhuman.'

Seneca's best known comments on the games were written after he had himself attended a munus. He deliberately avoided the morning animal hunts and timed his visit to coincide with the trained animal displays and the clowning about by the burlesque figures. Instead he blundered into the execution of condemned criminals. So disgusted was Seneca that he was moved to write:

> *It is pure murder. The men have no armour. They are exposed to blows at all points, and no one ever strikes in vain. Many prefer this event to the usual pairs (of gladiators) and to the bouts by request. Of course they do, there is no helmet or shield to deflect the weapon. What is the need of defensive armour or of skill? All these mean delaying death. In the morning they throw men to the lions and the bears: at noon they throw them to the spectators. The crowd demands that the slayer shall face the man who is to slay him in his turn; and they always reserve the latest killer for another killing. The outcome of every fight is death, and the means are fire and sword. This sort of thing goes on while the arena is empty. You may say 'But he was a mugger and he killed a man'. So what? Granted that, as a murderer, he deserved to die, but what crime have you committed that you should deserve to sit and watch? In the morning they cried 'kill him, lash him, burn him. Why does he stroke so feebly? Why doesn't he die well? Whip him to meet his wounds. Let them receive blow for blow, with chests bare and vulnerable to the blow'. Then the the games stop for the interlude and they announce 'A little throat slitting comes next so that there may still be something to watch.'*

Seneca's views and pronouncements had small impact. They had virtually none at all on the young Nero for he went on to become a great fan of the games. Seneca did however articulate a view held by a sizeable minority of Romans. The philosopher and historian Plutarch held government posts under Trajan and took the opportunity to write to provincial governors recommending that they should abolish gladiatorial combats in their jurisdiction. Most ignored him, though many did reduce the number of shows that took place.

About this same time, the two Greek cities of Athens and Corinth got embroiled in a furious rivalry. To demonstrate their superiority, the council of Athens decided to hold a great festival of art, literature and athletics, but also to include the Roman-style gladiatorial games. Introducing foreign activities was not popular with everybody and one Demonax declared in his speech 'Men of Athens, before you pass this rule you must destroy the Temple of Pity.'

Those pagans who objected to the gladiatorial bloodletting did so largely on the grounds that they corrupted those who watched them. The Christians had a different religion and a different way of looking at humanity. Christ specifically cared for people who were despised by society or were outcasts. He taught that respect and charity should be given to all humans.

The first Christian openly to denounce the slaughter in the arena was Tertullian, a writer from North Africa who practised as a lawyer in Rome before being converted to Christianity and returning to his home town to work as a preacher. He roundly condemned the games, writing 'he who shudders at the body of a fellow man who died a natural death common to all will, in the amphitheatre, gaze down with the most tolerant eyes on the bodies of men mangled, torn to pieces and defiled. Yes and he who comes to the spectacle to signify his approval of murder being punished will have a reluctant gladiator hounded on with lash and rod to do more murder.'

Even so the main thrust of Tertullian's writing was that the games should be banned because of the effect they had on the watching crowds rather than because of the cruelty of what went on in the arena.

Even the great Christian Augustine of Hippo was more worried about the effect the games had on the viewer than on the hapless men dying in the sand. He wrote about a young friend of his named Alypius who went to Rome to study law. One day this virtuous young Christian met some pagan friends in the street after lunch. They were off to the Colosseum to watch a gladiatorial combat and invited Alypius to join them. He refused, but they dragged him off with them anyway. Alypius declared 'You can drag my body there, but don't imagine that you can make me watch. Though I shall be there, I shall not be there. In this way I shall have the better of you and of your show.' The group of friends found seats, but Alypius sat with his eyes firmly shut. Augustine takes up the story:

In the course of the fight a man fell and there was a great roar from the vast crowd of spectators which struck his ears. He was overcome by curiosity and opened his eyes, perfectly prepared to treat whatever he might see with scorn. He saw the blood and he gulped down savagery. Far from turning away, he fixed his eyes on it. Without knowing what was happening, he drank in madness, he was delighted with the contest, drunk with the lust of blood. He was no longer the man who had come there, but was one of the mob. He was a true companion to those who had brought him. There is little more to be said. He looked, he shouted, he raved. He took away with him madness which would goad him to come back again and again. And he would not only come with those who first got him there, but would drag others with him.

It is interesting to note what Augustine says about the effect all this had on young Alypius. 'He received in his soul a worse wound than the glad-iator had received in his body. His own fall was more wretched than that of the man which had caused all the shouting that caused him to open his eyes and so made an opening of for the thrust which was to overpower his soul.' Augustine is still more worried about how a good Christian can be led astray than by the suffering of the pagan gladiator.

Whatever their motives and no matter how strongly they disap-proved of the *munera*, Christian writers were powerless in the face of official government support for the bloodshed. That changed in the early fourth century when Constantine the Great became Emperor. Constantine was declared emperor in AD 306, but it was not until AD 324 that he gained control of the entire empire, having defeated his rivals.

Although a pagan at this time, Constantine was supportive of the Christian church and recognized its growing power and influence in his empire. One of his first acts was to summon a great council of Christian bishops at Nicaea to sort out various doctrinal disputes that were causing troubles within the Church. The most famous result of this council was the Nicaean Creed, still repeated in Christian churches around the world. A less familiar result was the Edict of Berytus (Beirut) issued by Constantine.

The Edict of Berytus was concerned with the punishment of criminals. Among the provisions was the stipulation that magistrates must no longer send convicted criminals to serve as gladiators. Instead they were to be sent to work as slave labour in the mines. The conditions in the mines were frightful and death rates high, so leniency was probably not the motivation. The key to the new instruction is that the Edict also forbade the holding of gladiatorial games altogether. This order was undoubtedly issued under the influence of the Christian council. However as soon as the bishops had dispersed, Constantine was granting exemptions to various towns and cities, allowing them to continue to hold munera. In any case, the order never applied in Rome itself.

After Constantine's death in AD 337 many of his laws were ignored, the Edict of Berytus among them. By AD 357 the games were flourishing again across the Empire. In that year the Emperor Constantius II issued a military order forbidding serving soldiers from taking any part at all in gladiatorial games, including acting in their traditional role as guards. Clearly official disapproval of the games was growing, but just as clearly they were continuing to be held.

Meanwhile, in AD 366, the new Pope Damasus I intervened in a most unlikely fashion. The papal election held on the death of Liberius was hotly contested between Damasus and Ursinus, who had been secretary to Liberius. Damasus won a majority, but Ursinus got to the Church first and had himself crowned as Pope before barricading himself inside the Julian Basilica along with his supporters. Damasus then rounded up his backers and marched off to the gladiatorial training school near the Colosseum. There he hired the gladiators and sent them to the basilica to oust Ursinus. The gladiators were, of course, good at such work. They killed 137 people and Ursinus fled, leaving Damasus as undisputed Pope.

The idea of gladiatorial contests as a suitable public entertainment was, however, slowly fading. The practice died in the eastern provinces first. They had never been as popular in the Greek-speaking part of the empire as in the Latin-speaking west. The idea of the gladiator had developed in Rome and spread out from there, now it was shrinking back. The last known gladiatorial munus in the Eastern provinces was held in Antioch in AD 392.

In Rome the games persisted unabated. It was in the 390s that

Augustine's friend Alypius was studying in Rome. In AD 404 came what is recognized as a seminal event. A munus was taking place in the Colosseum. The fight between a pair of gladiators had been announced and they had taken their places in the arena when there was a sudden commotion. Scrambling down the sheer wall from the seating areas was a Christian monk, later discovered to be Telemachus from Asia Minor.

The monk ran towards the gladiators to remonstrate with them on the subject of Christian brotherly love. He was intercepted by one of the attendants. Then a section of the crowd followed the monk into the arena and fighting broke out, leading to a riot in which Telemachus was one of the fatal victims.

The Emperor at the time was the devoutly Christian Honorius, then not yet twenty years old. Appalled by the death of a saintly monk, Honorius banned the gladiatorial games in Rome. They clearly continued elsewhere, however, for after the Emperor's death in AD 423 the new ruler, Valentinian III allowed the games back to the Colosseum. By this date the barbarians were raging through the empire and keeping a precise chronology of consuls and their works was a low priority. Rome had been sacked by the Visigoths in AD 410, the Vandals were in Spain and the Germans were looting Gaul.

Amid this chaos one consul held a gladiatorial games some time in the later 420s, and had a celebratory medal struck to commemorate the event. Another consul had a similar medal struck in the 430s and we have a vague record of gladiatorial games being fought in Rome in the 440s. By this date the Roman Empire was in terminal decline. The Eastern Provinces had their own Emperor in Constantinople, now Istanbul, and the barbarians had carved up the Western Provinces between them. The title of Emperor of Rome was little more than a bauble to legitimize the naked military power of whichever barbarian king could grab it.

In such circumstances nobody any longer had the power or the inclination to hold gladiatorial games. The Roman mob no longer had any real say in how power was distributed or maintained, so there was little point in buying their support. In any case, the bloodthirsty fights were no longer as popular as they had been. The city was becoming increasingly Christian and the Church was doing its best to ban the bloodletting.

Some time after AD 440 the gladiatorial games stopped altogether.

PART II
CIRCUSES

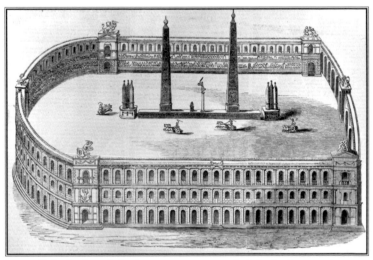

Originally built of wood, the Circus Maximus was rebuilt by the Emperor Augustus around 30 BC after it was destroyed by fire. The new circus was 2,000 feet long by 380 feet wide, and provided seating for almost 150,000 people, larger than any modern football stadium.

I

˒ THE CIRCUS ˒

BETWEEN THE PALATINE AND AVENTINE HILLS, close to the banks of the Tiber, lay an open valley. The valley was about 600 yards long and varied between 120 and 150 yards wide. Along the centre flowed a small stream which rose on the Esquiline Hill and fell into the Tiber at the valley's northern end. Before Rome was built, this valley was overgrown with wild myrtle and formed a sheltered spot for shepherds and travellers to rest. At the north-eastern corner of the valley there was a small stone altar to perhaps the oldest deity in the Roman pantheon: Murcia. It must have been a tranquil valley indeed for Murcia was the goddess of laziness and relaxation; she can have had no idea what was to happen to her beautiful valley.

While Rome was a collection of huts on the hilltops, the steep slopes of the Palatine Hill provided a ready made bank on which spectators could lounge to watch festivals and shows taking place on the grassy meadow on the floor of Murcia's Valley. There was space for tens of thousands of people on the Palatine slopes, and as many again could sit on the Esquiline. For centuries the entire population of Rome could turn out here to watch parades, processions, religious rituals and celebrations of all kinds.

On the slopes above the stream, near the summit of the Palatine, the earliest Romans built a series of stone-lined storage pits in which the grain harvest was placed for safekeeping over the winter. Here was built a small temple to the god Consus, patron of the harvest.

PART II: CIRCUSES

Legend has it that Romulus, the founder of Rome, organized a horse race to honour Consus and invited the neighbouring Sabines to attend. The Romans used the distraction of the race to give themselves the opportunity to kidnap the unmarried daughters of the Sabines, whom they later married in order to avert a war.

So the Valley of Murcia was associated with horse racing from the earliest legendary times of Romulus and over the years was transformed into the Circus Maximus. Popular and dramatic as the gladiatorial games may have been, they were not the only entertainment on offer to the Roman mob. For sheer ostentation, scale, luxury and expense they were simply dwarfed by what went on at the Circus, the largest and most magnificent public arena in Rome.

The first signs that the valley in its natural state was no longer good enough for Rome came in the reign of King Tarquinius Priscus, the fifth King of Rome who traditionally reigned from 616 BC to 578 BC. Priscus built temporary wooden platforms on which the senators could place their chairs and tables while watching events in the valley. The remaining citizens still sat on the grass. In 329 BC these wooden platforms were made permanent with the erection of very solid timber platforms and decking.

In 189 BC the small stream along the centre of the valley was covered over by a stone vaulted drain. The line of the hidden stream was marked by the stone roof of the drain on which was put a statue of Pollentia and other minor deities. This stone ridge was to become the *spina*, the central axis of the developing Circus Maximus. Fifteen years later the censors Quintus Fulvius Flaccus and Postumius Albinus rebuilt the spina, making it a tall structure in its own right, not just a drain cover, and erected stone seating for the senators and for the first time gave the general populace wooden seating.

By this date the Circus Maximus was being used extensively for chariot racing, so Flaccus and Albinus included in their rebuilding of the spina seven large eggs of wood. These were mounted on a stand so that they could be made to fall one after the other to count the laps run by the racing chariots. The innovation was so successful that the eggs were soon joined by seven dolphins which operated in a similar fashion.

The two censors introduced another important innovation regarding the organisation of the races. Previously the chariots had lined up at the northern end of the arena while awaiting the start, signalled by the presiding magistrate waving in his hand a *mappa*, or sacred and embroidered cloth. This procedure had led to several false starts and accusations of cheating. There were also serious problems caused by the jittery horses making each other nervous and so disrupting the start of the race.

Flaccus and Albinus found the answer in what became known as *carceres*. Although they were later to become highly elaborate structures, the carceres of 189 BC were simple wooden sheds with a door at each end. There were twelve carceres in the Circus Maximus, one for each chariot team in even the largest races. A chariot would enter at the rear and the doors would be closed behind it. In front of the horses was a thick rope strung at the height of their chests which stopped them from leaving the shed.

The wooden panelling on either side of the carceres stopped the horses from becoming agitated by the rival teams, while the rope physically blocked any attempts at an early start. When the presiding magistrate gave the signal to start the race, a lever was pulled which brought the ropes down to the ground simultaneously, allowing the charioteers to drive their steeds forward.

The long narrow shape of the Valley of Murcia made it necessary for the chariots to race several times around the spina, usually seven, to produce a race of a reasonable length. This layout of race course, which developed in the Circus merely because of the shape of the valley, was to become standard throughout the empire, other circuses being built to this plan even in Rome itself.

In 31 BC the Circus Maximus caught fire. All the wooden structures were utterly destroyed and the stone buildings were severely damaged. The following year the Emperor Augustus returned to Rome having defeated Anthony and Cleopatra and reunited the entire Roman Empire under his own rule. As one of the moves in his assumption of power, Augustus decided to rebuild the Circus Maximus completely, thus hopefully winning the support of the people and consolidating his popularity.

The Circus that Augustus built fitted into the Valley of Murcia, but was an entirely artificial structure which did not rely on the hillsides for support. It was almost 2,000 feet long and 380 feet wide and stood two storeys high. The ground floor was of stone and contained shops facing outward. The upper storey was of wood and contained the stairs and passages by which the crowd gained access to the banked seating, facing inward. Although a special podium was erected for the Emperor and his honoured guests, the seating was designed so that the Imperial palace on the Palatine Hill had a good view of the arena below. In all the Circus offered seating for about 150,000 people.

The northern end of the track was straight and contained the carceres from which the chariots emerged at the start of races. The southern end was rounded to allow space for the chariots to turn. Because processions traditionally passed down the Valley of Murcia, a gateway was provided at the southern end that led through the banks of seating. On the spina, Augustus erected an Egyptian obelisk to mark his conquest of Cleopatra. The entire building was faced with marble, inside and out, thus helping to justify the famous boast of Augustus that 'I found Rome a city of brick, but left it a city of marble.'

Over the years that followed, the mighty Circus Maximus was altered or renovated many times, but the basic structure of Augustus remained. Claudius rebuilt the carceres in marble and faced them with gilded statues while Nero installed luxurious seating for the knights, who ranked just below the senators in Roman society. Nero added some typically graceful touches with bronze dolphins which spouted water from their mouths into basins of water along the spina where the original stream flowed underground. At the southern end the gate by which processions left was taken down and replaced by a magnificent marble arch to honour the victory over the Jews by the Emperor Titus.

At the end of the first century AD the wooden upper storeys were damaged by fire. Rebuilt by Trajan, the Circus could now hold 250,000 spectators. This increase was achieved by extending the seating up to a third storey and outward, resting on arches built over and in front of the shops. These shops were, by this time, rather disreputable. As well as selling hot food and snacks, they were also home to prostitutes and astrologers. Trajan threw these characters out, though they soon returned.

The northern end of the Circus was remodelled to resemble a fortified gateway. On the outside were erected battlements and tall towers, which created a suitably impressive gateway through which sacred processions could enter the Circus. On the inside, the northern end had a special box in which sat the magistrate who controlled the races and his guests. The carceres were now positioned underneath this structure, so that they were roofed for the first time. This meant that the charioteers could no longer see when the magistrate was standing up and preparing to wave his mappa to start the race. To allow the drivers to prepare for the off, therefore, a trumpeter was stationed in the arena to blast out a fanfare as the man stood up.

The carceres were also equipped with wooden gates so that the horses were faced with blank wooden panels before the race began. The solid wooden gates were connected to powerful springs made of twisted sinews or ropes which would pull the doors open with tremendous force. The gates were held shut by metal bolts. An ingenious system of lever and hinges ensured that all the bolts were pulled back at the same instant to open the gates and so start the race.

Between the individual carceres were erected Greek-style *hermae*. These were stylized statues of the god Hermes which were used to mark boundaries and, by extension, doorways. Hermes is best known for being the messenger of the gods, but he was also a god of good luck in business and of fertility in animals. The Romans identified Hermes with their own god Mercury, the patron god of businessmen, whose main temple stood on the Esquiline Hill, just above the Circus Maximus. By the time they were installed at the Circus Maximus, the hermae were little more than a square pillar, tapering down to the base, topped by a head of the god and with an erect phallus halfway up the front. No doubt they were seen as being associated with good luck, animals and with the location.

The building underwent another major refurbishment in the reign of Constantius II in the 350s. This emperor was notoriously vain, loving ostentatious display and luxury in both his personal and his public life. He dragged from the sacred Egyptian city of Heliopolis an obelisk even larger than that erected by Augustus. He added to the spina marble reliefs of himself and other emperors conquering barbarian foes.

Bizarrely to modern eyes, but for perfectly valid Roman reasons, the whole history of the Circus Maximus saw one consistent feature that never altered. The little altar of Murcia remained ensconced amid the pomp and pageantry. The seating and apparatus of the Circus Maximus were built around the altar, which was protected by a low wall. Over the years the altar was repaired many times, but never removed or replaced. Later Romans could not recall who Murcia was nor why she was so revered. They thought she might be a manifestation of Venus, to whom the myrtle bush was sacred. Not until Christian times did the tiny shrine, which by then was over a thousand years old, become the target for destruction.

The altar of Murcia, like most of the Circus Maximus, was pillaged for building stone in medieval times. All that remains now is an open space surrounded by busy main roads.

II

˒ CHARIOT RACING ˒

POSSIBLY THE OLDEST and certainly the most popular sport in Rome was chariot racing. Fortunes were won and lost by betting on the races. Successful charioteers earned themselves vast wealth and huge estates by their victories, but losers were treated as worthless – or mangled to death by the speeding chariots of the victors. The Romans viewed the dramatic races of the Circus as a peculiarly Roman invention. And yet the first Romans knew nothing of the chariot, still less of racing.

All the earliest accounts of Rome agree that there were no chariots in the young kingdom. Men fought on foot or rode horses to battle, but of the chariot there is no mention in any of the early sources. The oldest chariot so far found in central Italy was in a tomb in Regolini dating to about 650 BC. The vehicle seems to have come from Greece, where chariots had been abandoned as a weapon of war about three centuries earlier, but were retained for ceremonial purposes and to allow a commander to get about the battlefield at speed. It was in the ceremonial role that they came to Italy, the early Romans using them in their triumphal processions.

The idea of racing lightweight chariots against each other seems to have emerged across central Italy in the sixth century BC, though whether it originated in Rome itself or somewhere else we have no way of knowing. Throughout central Italy, chariot and horse racing were held to be sacred to agricultural deities. Romulus, the founder of Rome, held a

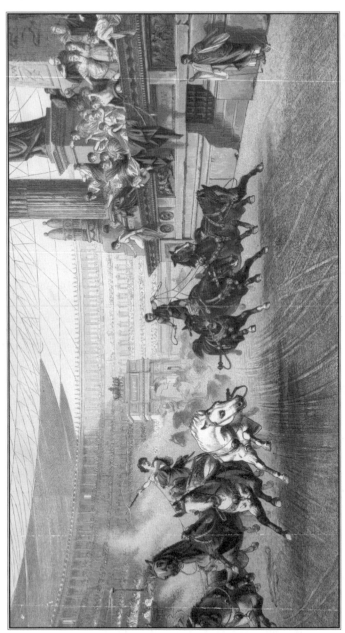

The Chariot Race. The four teams, or *factiones* of charioteers in Rome, the Reds, Blues, Greens and Whites attracted fanatical support from the populace. Here the Reds appear to have the upper hand.

horse race in honour of the god Consus, patron of the harvest. Other races were held to honour Segesta, goddess of growing crops, and Ceres, goddess of corn. The original religious significance of the races has been lost, but was probably linked to rejuvenating the fertility of these deities. Equally obscure is the date at which chariot racing replaced horse racing in the ceremonies.

At first the chariots, horses and drivers were provided by the Roman knights, the lesser nobility who were citizens of wealth but who lacked aristocratic ancestry. Participation in the race was a religious duty which helped to ensure the future prosperity of the city. Later men were more concerned with winning and began to hire professional charioteers, or buy them if they were slaves. By the time the chariot races were first recorded in any great detail the earlier freelance drivers and team owners had been replaced by two large and wealthy teams, known as *factiones*, which were known by their colours: White and Red. About 30 BC the Green faction was established and soon afterwards the Blues made an appearance. In the eighties AD the Emperor Domitian oversaw the establishment of two more factiones, the Purples and the Golds, but these new teams failed to attract much support among Romans and soon vanished.

Each factione had its own stables to the north of Rome on the Campus Martius, originally an army training ground, where the horses and chariots were kept for immediate use in the Circus. Further from Rome were the studs for breeding horses and the training grounds where horse and charioteers learned and practised their trade. There were also club houses where the supporters of a factione could gather to chat about drivers, horses and races. The club houses were sumptuously fitted out with high quality mosaics, wall paintings and furniture in the rooms for prestige citizens and more basic equipment for the rooms frequented by freemen and slaves.

Just about everyone in Rome supported one factione or another, and followed their team with fanatical devotion. Bets were laid between supporters and fans. As the crowd waited for the races to take place, they sang songs of encouragement for their faction and waved pieces of cloth of the appropriate colour. The crowd devised patterns of cloth waving so that ripples of colour eddied and swirled across the massed ranks of spectators in the Circus. On the terraces of the Circus Maximus the din of cheering and heckling was deafening as the horses thundered round the course. Grown men fainted when their team lost, shouted instructions to a charioteer that could not possibly be heard and hurled abuse at rivals. As the race neared its climax, fights might break out between rival fans or spectators might stand stupefied and silent as their teams won or lost.

The few people outside the Circus on race days could tell how the races were going by listening to the chanting and singing which drifted over the city from the hundreds of thousands of voices at the race track. In the second century AD one rich supporter of the Greens took to caging wild birds and colouring their faces green. If his team won the day, the birds were released so that everyone who saw them would know the Greens had been victorious.

Visiting Greeks have left several puzzled accounts of the behaviour of the Romans at chariot racing. In Greece it was the skill of the charioteer or the speed of the horses which brought forth applause or condemnation. In Rome it was the success or failure of the factione. Greeks found it difficult to understand how a charioteer could be lionized by their Roman host one day, then abused the next when he signed a contract with a different factione. Charioteers were public figures whose lives, relatives and likes were known to everyone in Rome. The desire for news of the top charioteers was insatiable, so that even humble stablehands were honoured dinner guests if they brought fresh gossip.

Outsiders found it almost impossible to understand the Roman devotion to chariot factiones and the thirst for news about their drivers and horses. In these days of football fan clubs and celebrity magazines it is, perhaps, easier to sympathize with what drove the Romans.

The centre of all this adulation, excitement and gossip was what went on in the Circus. The chariots used in the races were unlike the vehicles used for other purposes. The ceremonial chariots were large, heavy affairs decorated with gilded paintings and carrying several people at once. The racing chariot was stripped down to its barest essentials and carried just one man at high speeds.

The chariot wheels were small, barely eighteen inches in diameter and made of a wooden rim set on six or eight spokes and surrounded by an iron tyre. The wheels revolved freely on a fixed axle made of a single piece of timber. The five foot long axle ran from one wheel to the other and was connected to the chariot pole which ran forwards to the horses. Mounted on the junction of axle and pole was a wooden platform about two feet by eighteen inches on which stood the charioteer. Rising from the front of the platform was a wooden hoop which came up to the charioteer's waist. The open face of the hoop was filled in with leather or cloth dyed to the colour of the faction. This design gave a wide wheel base and low centre of gravity, making the chariot stable and unlikely to overturn on the sharp corners at either end of the Circus. There were, of course, no brakes. The charioteer relied entirely on the horses for acceleration or slowing down.

The chariot pole came out of the front of the chariot at an angle, sweeping upwards to reach the horses' shoulders. The horses either side of the pole wore a simple harness consisting of a girth around their stomachs and a chest band running forwards from the girth. This harness was connected to a short wooden yoke projecting from the sides of the pole which rested on the horses' shoulders. Additional horses wore a similar harness, but were linked to the pole by yoke.

The racing chariots were built for lightness, and considerable skill and technical innovation went into their construction. The Empire was scoured for the finest materials and the best craftsmen to be brought to Rome. It is thought that the chariots weighed as little as fifty-five pounds, which is astonishingly light for a vehicle made before the advent of modern polymers. Given that the races were held on flat, level ground this light weight can have done little to slow down the horses from their top speed.

All racing chariots were effectively identical in design and construction. It is true there were different categories used in different races but these were distinguished more by how many horses pulled the chariots rather than by the design of the chariots themselves. The usual format was the *quadriga*, which was drawn by four horses harnessed to the yoke abreast, with two horses either side of the pole. Almost as popular was the *biga*, or two-horse chariot. Although slightly slower, the biga was more manoeuvrable and could display the charioteer's skills to greater effect. The *triga*, or three horse chariot, was used only in the sacred races held to honour Ceres, the goddess of grain, and was never seen in races held for sport.

There are written records of *seiuga* and *octoiuga*, drawn by six and eight horses respectively. However the starting gates at the Circus Maximus and other racecourses were too small for such vehicles. They cannot have been used often and must have commenced their races from in front of the starting gates used for quadrigae. We know of at least one race held between chariots pulled by twenty horses each. These teams would have been far too cumbersome for speed racing and were probably used more to show off the skills of the driver than for any real sporting purpose.

The horses used to pull the chariots at first were the domestic horses of Roman gentry pitted against each other in sport or for religious purposes. Before long however, horses well suited to chariot racing were being bred and by the time the factiones had control of the sport horse breeding was a major industry in itself.

The best stallions – chariot racing was an almost exclusively male occupation among horses – came from North Africa and Spain. The studs of Greece and Asia Minor had their supporters, but they provided fewer horses to Rome than did the western provinces. The chariot horses were highly-prized creatures. Those that were successful in the Circus could look forward to many years of honourable retirement at stud, followed by a formal funeral and a proper grave. 'Sired on the sandy plains of Gaetulia, fast as the wind, unmatched in life, you now dwell in the realm of the gods' reads a typical gravestone erected to a chariot horse.

By studying the horse skeletons from these graves and careful analysis of the beautifully worked sculptures of chariot racing, modern equestrian experts have been able to produce a clear picture of the chariot horses of Rome. They stood about thirteen hands tall, around four and a half feet, which makes them slightly smaller than the modern riding horse, but puts them among the largest breeds of antiquity. They were fairly stocky animals with relatively short legs and large bodies compared to modern riding breeds. These features would have made them poor jumpers, but excellent runners, just the attributes needed for chariot racing. They are probably closest to the Andalusian of Spain among modern breeds of horse.

The horses could become the objects of a form of hero worship among the Roman crowds. The poet Martial, who died in AD 104, was a favourite at the court of the Emperors Domitian and Titus and mixed with the cream of Roman society. But even he was moved to complain at one point that 'I am known in all the provinces and to all the peoples of the Roman world, but in Rome I am less famous than the horse Andraemon'. Rich men decorated their houses with paintings and mosaics of favoured chariot horses. 'Win or lose I love you Polidox' are the words on one mosaic.

The charioteers, the *auriga*, were no less famous than the horses. No respectable Roman noble would have dreamed of driving a chariot team by the third century BC, nor at any time thereafter. Like prostitutes and gladiators, charioteers made a living with their entire bodies, rather than by a skill such as oratory or metalworking. In Roman eyes this robbed them of any social honour or dignity and would have made them automatically ineligible to stand in election or speak in public.

Instead the auriga were slaves, freemen and plebeians. Most of them originated as slaves or employees of the factiones. They would start off working as grooms or stableboys and begin driving at the country horse ranches where horses were trained and exercised. If they showed enough skill they could be promoted to being circus drivers. A few men came to the factiones as fully fledged chariot drivers from the provinces, but such freelancers were rare.

Driving techniques were very different from what might be expected. The charioteers did not stand on their chariots lashing the horses with a whip in one hand and reins in the other. Instead the charioteer tied the reins around his body, just below the arms. He then took up his stance on the chariot, bracing his legs against the upright wooden hoop and keeping a tight grip with one hand while his other wielded the whip. To encourage the horses to move forwards, the auriga would lean forward, slackening the reins. To brake he would lean back, drawing the reins tight. Making the horses turn was accomplished by leaning to one side or the other. Only in the most desperate circumstances would the driver take his hand off the hoop to tug on the reins, for this would make it dangerously easy for him to lose his balance and tumble out of the chariot.

Accidents were frequent and no doubt added to the excitement of the sport. Tumbles and trippings seem to have been common, but a total crash was not unknown and went by the name of *naufragium*, or shipwreck. One such accident was recorded by a writer in the fifth century 'His horses were brought down, a multitude of intruding legs entered the wheels, and the twelve spokes were crowded, until a crackle came from those crammed spaces and the revolving rim shattered the entangled feet; then he, a fifth victim, flung from his chariot, which fell upon him, caused a mountain of manifold havoc, and blood disfigured his prostrate brow.'

The charioteers were, of course, at risk of serious injury in such accidents. To give themselves some protection they wore small, round helmets made up of layer upon layer of tough leather which was held in place by a chin strap. The body was encased in tough leather armour and the limbs tightly bound with leather over cloth padding.

By tying the reins around his body, the charioteer gave himself tight control of the horses, but risked being dragged to his death in the event of a crash. All drivers carried a short, curved knife tucked into their costume so that they would be able to cut themselves free.

The gravestones of some of them have survived and give details of the men and their careers. Gaius Appuleius Diocles, for instance, retired from racing at the age of forty-two after more than two decades as a charioteer. In that time he won no less than 1,462 races and took part in an amazing 4,257.

Less fortunate was the auriga whose tomb carries the inscription 'Marcus Aurelius Polyneices, born a slave, lived twenty-nine years, nine months, five days. Won the palm 739 times, 655 times for the Reds, 55 for the Greens, 12 for the Blues and 17 for the Whites. Killed driving.'

The records of individual charioteers show a clear pattern. Like Polyneices, they usually have a few victories for each of three factiones, but the vast majority of victories are won for a particular Colour. The implication would seem to be that early in a driver's career he might chop and change between teams with ease, but that once he began to become successful he would stay with one Colour for the rest of his days. Only rarely do we see records of men who seem to have moved from one Colour to another at the height of their success. It did happen, however, for we know that famous drivers could be abused in the street by fans of the factione they had abandoned.

The drivers could became fantastically wealthy, in the manner of some modern sports stars. The big races run at major festivals in the Circus Maximus at Rome paid fabulous prizes to the winners. These sums of money averaged about 20,000 sesterce for each race, with especially prestigious contests paying out 60,000 sesterce. This was at a time when the pay of a soldier in Rome's legions was around twenty sesterce per week and most citizens in Rome would have expected to earn much the same. The charioteers had to pay a sizeable part of their winnings to the factione for the upkeep of horses and chariots, but even so the successful driver usually ended up a wealthy man.

The races themselves conformed to a set pattern which was rigorously followed. First the factiones would cast lots to decide which team started from which *carceres*. The chariots would then be harnessed up and led into the starting stalls.

The writer Sidonius Apollinaris describes the scene as the charioteers wait for the start. 'There behind the barriers chafe those beasts, pressing against the fastenings, while a vapoury blast comes forth between the wooden bars and even before the race the field they have not yet entered is filled with their panting breath...never are their feet still, but restlessly they lash the hardened timber....The others are busy with hand and voice, and everywhere the sweat of drivers and flying steeds falls in drops on to the field. The hoarse roar from applauding partisans stirs the heart, and the contestants, both horse and men, are warmed by the race and chilled by fear.'

When the magistrate threw down his white cloth, the doors to the carceres would fly open and the charioteers lash their teams out to reach a gallop as quickly as possible. The teams emerged onto the broad area at the northern, or square end, of the Circus. Races were run anti-clockwise, so the teams had to pass to the right side of the spina, or central stone divide running down the middle of the Circus. A white line was marked on the sand between the spina and the outside edge of the race track. The race itself started at this line, not when the chariots emerged from the carceres. The distance between the two was to give the charioteers a chance to pick up speed, but not to change position or jostle an opponent.

Virgil wrote about the start of a race 'See you not, when in headlong contest the chariots have seized upon the plain, and stream in a torrent from the barrier, when the young driver's hopes are high, and throbbing fear drains each bounding heart? On they press with circling lash, bending forward to slacken rein; fiercely flies the glowing wheel. Now sinking low, now raised aloft, they seem to be borne through empty air and to soar skyward. No rest, no stay is there; but a cloud of yellow sand mounts aloft, and they are wet with the foam and the breath of those in pursuit...'

Once across the line, however, the aurigae could behave pretty much as they liked. They were free to choose the route that suited them best, to cut in front of rivals or to set their own horses to crowd out another team. The trick was to be able to turn the sharp hairpin bends at either end of the track at as great a speed as possible and keep tightly close to the spina. As the teams turned, the light chariots would skid sideways on, bump and slide over the sand. Drivers tried to push each other off the best line and squeeze their teams in to any available gap.

The total distance of seven laps around the Circus Maximus is almost three miles and races lasted about ten minutes. This equates to an average speed of some 21 mph. This is fairly slow for a galloping horse, but the teams must have had to slow down considerably to take the corners, speeding up again for the long straight runs.

After the race the losing teams quietly exited the Circus, but the winner drove to the podium where the presiding magistrate sat. The driver approached the podium to collect his palm of victory and his prize money. The winning chariot was then decorated with laurels and the charioteer set off on a lap of honour before leaving to return to his stables.

There is one aspect of the chariot racing which remains something of a mystery. Many mosaics and reliefs of the racing show men mounted on horses galloping alongside the chariots. These men wear the same sort of protective clothing as the charioteers and are likewise dressed in tunics dyed with their team colours. In some depictions these riders are labelled *hortatores*. There seems to have been one such rider for each factione irrespective of how many chariots were taking part in the race. The riders are not, however, mentioned in written sources. Who they were and what their role was is quite unknown.

III

ꞏ ROMAN FESTIVALS ꞏ

I N THE EARLY CENTURIES OF ROME the Circus Maximus was large enough to seat the entire population of the city. Even in the later centuries when more than a million people lived in Rome, the Circus could provide seating for all the citizens at least. This made it the natural venue for any large scale celebration, display or festival. If a thing was worth doing, it was worth doing in the Circus.

Among the many events in the public life of Rome to be celebrated in the Circus, at least in part, were the great festivals – the *ludi*. These public holidays were held on set dates throughout the year, though they were sometimes moved for religious or political reasons. Some of the ludi were as old as Rome itself, others were introduced over the years as new gods, new tastes and new fashions came to the city from its expanding empire.

The public holidays and festivals – the ludi – were celebrated in grand style and were considered by the Romans to be one of the main benefits of living in the city. The spectacular shows and meals that featured in most of the public festivals were provided free of charge to citizens. In Roman religion it was considered absolutely essential that the public festivals, or at least their sacred content, was carried out perfectly and punctually. The gods honoured in the festivals were thought to be seriously displeased by any lapse in ceremonial or ritual that occurred. And the anger of the gods was something of which the Romans were very afraid.

Saturn devours his children. Saturn, the Roman god of agriculture, was originally the Father of the senior Roman gods Jupiter, Neptune and Pluto. With the introduction of agriculture he began a period of peace and prosperity – the Golden Age. The Roman festival of the harvest, Saturnalia, is in mid December and Saturday is named for him. From the 3rd century he was identified with the Greek Kronos; fated to be overthrown by one of his children, he tried to prevent this by eating his children at birth.

The only way to ensure that the correct sacrifices were made in the correct ritual on the correct day was for the state to organize them. It might be the priests of the different temples who played a central role in the rituals, but it was government officials who organized the equipment and people to be ready on time.

The officials to whom these duties were given were the Aediles. There were originally two Aediles who seem to have been secular officials at the Temple of Ceres, the corn goddess, which was called the Aedes. In 367 BC the office was made elective by the whole citizenry and the number of Aediles increased to four. The Aediles supervised the public life of Rome in the streets. They were responsible for cleaning the streets, repairing public buildings, ensuring market traders used accurate weights and that the public festivals passed off without a problem. If any malfunction did occur, the festivals would need to be staged again.

The Aediles soon learned that they could manipulate their office to improve their chances of being elected to more senior positions in future years. If they organized festivals which not only pleased the gods, but also pleased the voting public the Aediles could gather supporters and votes. The funds provided by the state could be used by the Aediles to put on adequate shows, but to make a real impression the Aediles had to dip into their own pockets. Being an Aedile could be a hugely expensive business and more than one man found himself almost bankrupted by his year in office. The money spent on being Aedile was often, however, a worthwhile investment. If the man went on to hold one of the more lucrative political posts he would be able to recoup his investment and pay back any money he had borrowed.

It was the competition between Aediles that led to the various festivals becoming increasingly extravagant and sumptuous. Chariot-racing in the Circus was, at first, part of only a few of the ludi but it proved to be very popular. Therefore despite the colossal expense of staging them, chariot races gradually became a part of nearly every festival. So ubiquitous did they become that Romans started referring to the public entertainments of the ludi as being 'circuses'.

Another way for the Aediles to court popularity was to create new festivals or extend existing ones. The usual pretext for new holidays was a vow to a god. This might be a promise to hold games if a drought ended or if there was a good harvest. These votive games were usually held just once though a few came to be held off and on for several years. Other Aediles took advantage of family affairs to court favour. If a venerable relative died while the Aedile was in office, a suitably impressive *munus*, a gladiatorial show, could be staged. Some aspiring politicians put off the munus they owed a dead relative until such time as they held the Aedileship.

The various extensions of festivals, imposition of new festivals and other contortions of the ritual calendar made by successive Aediles had an impact on the Roman calender. By 50 BC the calendar was about 100 days out of synchronisation with the seasons, so festivals nominally associated with the harvest were being held long after the crops had been gathered in. In 45 BC, Julius Caesar introduced a new calendar, the Julian Calendar which not only put the festivals back in touch with the seasons, but also introduced leap years and months of varying length.

The Romans themselves liked to give the credit for many of their festivals to a man called Evander. According to legend, Evander was a son of the Greek prophetess Carmente and the god Hermes, though no such son is known to Greek legend. He was reputed to have come to Italy about the time of the Trojan wars and founded the village of Pallanteum, from which the Palatine Hill later took its name. Evander is credited with having introduced many aspects of Greek culture, such as writing and the worship of various gods, to Italy. By about 200 BC, the Romans were willing to give credit to Evander for just about anything which was so old that its true origins had been lost to history.

One of the things credited to Evander was the idea of holding games to celebrate the festivals of the gods. In particular, the habit of holding equestrian games to honour agricultural deities is said to have come from this ancient Greek. The oldest of these festivals, and the one most closely linked to the Circus, was the Ludus Consuales which were held in the middle of August as a sign that the grain harvest was to begin.

The first Ludus Consuales were held by Romulus in around 740 BC. According to legend, he discovered a miraculous underground altar sacred to the god Consus, patron of grain storage. Romulus held a series of horse races, then covered the altar with earth again until the following year. This habit of excavating and reburying the altar of Consus was continued through out the history of Rome. By about 100 BC it had led to this agricultural god being linked to secret advice and good counsel offered to government officials.

The Ludus Consuales, meanwhile, continued to be celebrated in their ancient fashion. On the day of the festival all horses, donkeys and mules in the city of Rome were given a day off from work by their masters. They were then adorned with garlands of laurel and with flowers before being led through the streets in a procession. Finally the crowds gathered at the Circus for a series of races. At first the races were between mounted nobles, but by around 400 BC were being run between chariots. So popular did the chariot races of the Ludus Consuales become that they were gradually grafted on to other holidays and festivals that, originally had nothing to do with either horses or agricultural gods.

One of the festivals to have acquired chariot racing rather late in its existence was the Ludi Maximi – the Great Games. The name of the festival refers not to its size or luxury, but to the fact that it was held to honour the powerful state god Jupiter. This mighty sky deity was the chief god of the Romans. He was believed to have led the other gods in a series of desperate wars against the Titans, the Giants and against the older deities led by Saturn. Emerging victorious, Jupiter gave the sea to his brother Neptune and the underworld to his other brother Pluto, keeping the sky and rule over the world to himself. He went on to father a whole family of gods and demi-gods, thus creating the Roman pantheon. The oak was sacred to Jupiter, as were white bulls. In origin, Jupiter is just one face of the ancient, all-powerful sky god worshipped by most Indo-European peoples under names such as Zeus, Odin and Woden.

In Rome, Jupiter was considered so mighty and majestic that it was thought improper for individual citizens to presume to offer him prayers or sacrifices. Only the citizens of Rome as a body could do so. The ceremonies held in Jupiter's honour were mostly solemn, so the Ludus Maximi no doubt came as a welcome piece of revelry amongst the earnest worship of this god of state. The games were founded by the fifth King of Rome, Tarquin Priscus, in about 590 BC, at least according to legend. At first they consisted of a military review to demonstrate the armed might of the city and the readiness of the citizens for war, but later mock combats between champions were added. Finally, chariot racing became a key feature of the festival and it moved from the Campus Martius to the Circus.

One of the most ancient of the Roman festivals was Lupercalia, held on 15 February. The Romans believed it had been established by Romulus, the founder of Rome, in honour of the wolf which had suckled him as a baby – the Latin for 'wolf' being 'lupus'. In later centuries the festival was dedicated to the god Pan. This god of the countryside was especially linked to hunters and could appear in the shape of a goat, or half-goat. In Greece, Pan had powers to improve fertility, which may explain why he became associated with this Roman festival.

The day of the Lupercalia began when two youths, always members of Roman noble families, walked to the Capitol dressed only in loin cloths and leading two goats and a dog. When they arrived they were met by two priests, the heads of the two ancient schools of priests, the Fabiani and Quintiliani. These schools were believed to have been founded by Romulus and Remus respectively. The priests then sacrificed the animals to Pan, wiping the blades of the sacrificial knives clean on the faces of the boys. The animals were skinned and rawhide whips made from the skins.

The two youths took the whips and ran through the streets of the city, lashing out at anyone they could reach with their bloody weapons. The boys were encouraged to whip women especially hard as the touch of the sacred whips was believed to ensure safe, painless and speedy childbirth. The festival ended only when the boys dropped from exhaustion.

As with many Roman festivals, the Lupercalia was touched by scandal. In 43 BC the place of one of the youths was taken by the grown man, Mark Anthony, then Consul of Rome. We are not sure why Anthony chose to break with tradition by taking the place normally filled by a beardless boy, but we do know that he was universally condemned for lowering the dignity of his high office by running almost naked through the city. Julius Caesar went on to make matters worse when he introduced a new college of priests, which he named the Julii in his own honour, and insisted that they take part in the Lupercalia. The populace of Rome, at least those who were more conservative in their beliefs, turned against the two friends.

Equally ancient was the Saturnalia, held at first on 19 December, but later extended to run until 25 December. The festival originated as a celebration of the winter crop sowing, but by 496 BC when it was enlarged on the orders of the dictator Posthumius after a victory over the Sabines, it was a general season of merry making.

Friends exchanged gifts with each other while all shops, businesses, schools and public offices were closed. It became traditional for executions to be postponed and for Roman armies in the field to seek temporary truces with the enemy so that the soldiers could enjoy the festival.

The unique feature of the Saturnalia was that slaves were able to speak to their masters, and to each other, on any subject they wished and could even take the opportunity to ask favours of free citizens. The eating, drinking, chariot-racing and general jollity of Saturnalia was so popular in Rome that when Christianity took over as the state religion many of its features were incorporated into the Christian festival of Christmas.

In contrast to the ancient festivals about which even the Romans were rather vague, some ludi had very definite beginnings. One of these was the Ludi Apollinares held in honour of the god Apollo.

In 212 BC Rome was in a terrible predicament. She was at war with the powerful North African city of Carthage, and was doing badly. The great Carthaginian general Hannibal had invaded Italy and in three great battles wiped out half of Rome's manpower. In the spring of 212 Hannibal was besieging allies of Rome in southern Italy, when he suddenly turned on Rome itself. He drew his army up for battle a mile or two outside the Colline Gate. The Romans marched out to face the invader, fearing greatly that they would be defeated. Suddenly a violent thunderstorm of hail hit the two armies, forcing them to seek shelter. The next day the same thing happened again. On the third day, Hannibal rode up to the walls of Rome with a scouting party. Glaring up at the soldiers manning the Colline Gate, Hannibal hurled his spear at them. The shaft passed overhead and rattled into the street beyond. Hannibal then learned that his forces in the south were doing badly and hurried off to assist them.

It had been a close thing for Rome. As usual in these circumstances the Romans consulted their books of prophecy and found that it had been foretold that Apollo would one day save Rome with his heavenly arrows. Taking the hailstorms to be Apollo's arrows, the Romans held the Ludi Apollinares on the anniversary of Hannibal's retreat. To symbolize their victory, the Romans wore laurel wreaths throughout the holiday. At first the festival was marked by music and theatre, both sacred to Apollo, but it was not long before the races at the Circus began to feature as well.

The Ludi Floralia, the games sacred to Flora the flower goddess, took place in April but were not held every year. Flora was originally a goddess of the Sabines, Rome's neighbours to the east in the Appenine Hills, but she was adopted by the Romans by about 500 BC and in 238 BC the Floralia was first held in Rome. Respectable Romans did not have much to do with this foreign cult for it was notorious for its pornographic content. Written accounts of exactly what went on are vague, but certainly naked female dancers formed a central part of the festival.

Another foreign goddess to dominate a Roman festival was Cybele who became the patron of the Ludi Megalenses. The cult of Cybele began in Asia Minor where she was said to be the mother of all the gods and where a stone which fell from the sky, presumably a meteorite, was her sacred symbol. The holy stone was brought to Rome in 204 BC and placed in a temple on the Palatine Hill, overlooking the Circus. Cybele was an earth mother goddess with powers of fertility and some impressive sexual appetites.

Her worship could be carried out only by eunuch priests and for many years citizens of Rome were forbidden to become priests of Cybele because of the ritual mutilation involved. Not until the reign of Claudius did the cult of Cybele become incorporated in the official calendar of Roman games when the Ludi Megalenses were expanded to last from 4 to 10 April and to include the by now almost obligatory chariot races.

There were many other ludi in the Roman calendar, some of which faded out of use and were then replaced by others. The Ludi Cereales, held in April, were enlivened by the custom that before the chariot races were run a number of foxes with burning torches attached to their tails were let loose in the Circus. The Ludi Plebeii were held in November to celebrate the wine harvest and were notoriously drunken affairs.

Perhaps the most unusual of the regular games were the Ludi Saeculares, held only once every hundred years, though after the festival of 17 BC the periods of time were altered somewhat and the festival held more erratically. The religious part of the festival took place at night when a solemn procession marched from the city gates to the Campus

Martius. Here the priests excavated an underground altar named Terentus, then slit the throats of a pair of black bulls, allowing the blood to run over the altar of the god of the dead and of the underworld. The altar was then carefully reburied and the ground smoothed over before the procession returned to the city. The public games could then begin.

During the period of the Empire, the duty of staging the public games was still, officially, in the hands of the Aediles. The emperors, however, made it very clear that it was they and their generosity that made the games possible. No emperor wanted an upstart young man taking the credit and acquiring power through the citizens' votes. But popular opinion is not so easily stifled. If the mob could not voice concerns through candidates and elections, they would soon find another way to make their feelings known.

Belisarius, the Byzantine general appointed by the emperor Justinian to defend the Eastern empire in its dying days. He successfully repelled the Persian invasion of AD 534, and reconquered Rome, Naples and Ravenna for Justinian. He also put down the 'Nike' riots of AD 532.

IV

ˎ THE GREAT RIOTS ˎ

THE EMPEROR DOMITIAN, who ruled from AD 81 to 96, was a great fan of the races, but did not much care for the mob. He had a wooden screen built around the Imperial seating area so that he could watch the races without being seen by the crowds. Domitian had reason to be careful, for his rule was unpopular and there were several conspiracies against him. 'A ruler is most unfortunate,' he once said, 'since when there is a conspiracy, nobody believes him unless he is killed'. But the mob did not like their emperor to hide himself. The popular discontent voiced by the mob in the Circus merely spurred on the would-be conspirators and they murdered Domitian in his bedroom.

The next emperor, Nerva, did not use the screened seats at the Circus, but his rule of two years ended in a natural death. His adopted successor, Trajan, tore down the wooden screens. The first time Trajan took his seat in the Imperial seats in full view of the crowds the cheering was loud and prolonged. The mob had their emperor back where they wanted him.

While the mob bayed their support or condemnation of policies in the Circus, the chariot racing *factiones* operated in more subtle manner. Most Romans belonged to one of the four factiones and the most senior men were welcome visitors at the luxurious clubs run by the different Colours. There a considerable amount of lobbying went on to try to secure government posts or contracts for the adherents of the different teams.

The best known example of such patronage came in the shape of

Aulus Vitellius, a driver for the Greens during the reign of Caligula. The dissolute emperor won much money by betting on Vitellius and brought him into the Imperial household as a favourite, though his official position seems to have been as a senior official in the stables. Vitellius managed to retain his post under Claudius, but with Nero he achieved high office through the simple stratagem of telling the new emperor what a superb musician he was. When Nero was overthrown and committed suicide, Vitellius survived because the commander of the Praetorian Guard, Tiberius Vinius, was a fellow member of the Greens Club. On the advice of Vinius the new emperor, Galba, appointed Vitellius Governor of the German frontier. Galba was soon afterwards murdered and replaced by Otho. Vitellius marched the legions of the German frontier on Rome, killed Otho and became Emperor.

Throughout the Empire the Circus factiones continued their political intrigues, as the mob continued to shout for action in the Circus. Gradually the Whites became subservient to the Greens and the Reds to the Blues. By around AD 300 there were two enormously wealthy and powerful sporting clubs or partnerships in Rome.

The rivalry soon began to acquire political connotations. The Blues had a large proportion of members from the old families of Rome and tended to attract support for tradition and more conservative measures. The Greens, in contrast, pulled their financial backing from wealthy provincials and the newly-rich. They tended to favour more radical political programmes. So long as the Emperors ruled firmly, if not well, the factiones did little more than lobby for influence and bay out insults. When the Emperors began to falter, however, the Circus teams took on a far more threatening attitude.

Each of the teams was run by a group of citizens known as the *domini factionum quadrigaria*. These men were drawn from the social class of *equite*, or knights, the lesser nobility of Rome. Each Colour had the power to decide its own composition, replacing one director with another as men died or retired. It is likely that new directors were expected to lavish money as well as time on the team for running a chariot factiones was an expensive business. Hundreds of men were employed directly and thousands more indirectly by each Colour. Close links were maintained with the factiones of the same colour in provincial towns. Although these were independent clubs, they shared facilities and personnel with the senior Colour in Rome. The factiones were wealthy, independent organisations which had contacts throughout the empire. If they chose to exercise their power, they could be dangerous.

In 455 the western Emperor Valentinian III ordered the murder of his general Aetius, who had defeated Attila the Hun, but was now suspected of becoming too ambitious. Two of Aetius' officers then killed Valentinian. The wealthy senators in Rome, with the support of the Blues, then elevated Senator Petronius Maximus to the throne. The Greens were unhappy and rioting broke out. Maximus tried to slip out of the city to bring the army in to restore order, but was hit on the head by a stone hurled from the mob. He fell unconscious and was killed. Over the following twenty years the mob, the Colours and the army quarrelled, rioted and fought over the occupancy of the imperial throne even as the power of that throne collapsed.

After there ceased to be an emperor in Rome at all, the chariot factiones remained powerful and active in politics. The political situation became hopelessly confused as barbarian kings, popes and the Senate all struggled to achieve and hold power. The Colours had their final fling in 509. After the death of Pope Anastasius II, Symmachus was elected Pope by a majority of the clergy in Rome at the time. His elevation was opposed by the Senate, still speaking for the rich men of central Italy, who persuaded some clergy to declare a priest named Lawrence to be Pope. Theodoric, King of the Ostrogoths, the largest barbarian tribe in Italy, stepped in to back Symmachus, but still the Senate refused to accept him.

Finally in 509, the city of Rome was torn apart by bloody rioting between the aristocratic Blues, backing Lawrence, and the plebeian Greens, backing Symmachus. The Greens won and Symmachus was firmly established as Pope.

These riots resulted from the heady blend of politics and Circus factions and the extremes to which they could go were shown by the famous Nike Riots of AD 532. They took place in Constantinople and have achieved great fame because they were recorded in detail by a contemporary. No doubts the riots that took place in Rome were similar in their fanaticism and violence, but the details have passed almost unrecorded.

On 1 January 532 a demonstration took place against new taxes introduced by a new Emperor, Justinian. The troops were sent in and the two ringleaders arrested and sentenced to death. Unfortunately for Justinian, one of the men was a prominent member of the Blues and the other an equally important Green. A contemporary account continues:

The members of the two factions conspiring together and declaring a truce with each other, seized the prisoners and then straightway entered the prison and released all those who were in confinement there. Fire was applied to the city as if it had fallen under the hand of an enemy. The emperor and his consort, with a few members of the senate shut themselves up in the palace and remained there. Now the watch-word which the populace passed to one another was Nike – meaning 'Victory'.

On the fifth day of the insurrection in the late afternoon the Emperor Justinian gave orders to Hypatius and Pompeius, nephews of the late emperor, Anastasius, to go home as quickly as possible, probably because he suspected that some plot was being matured by them against his own person. But they feared that the people would force them to the throne and they said that they would be doing wrong if they should abandon their sovereign when he found himself in such danger. When the Emperor Justinian heard this, he inclined still more to his suspicion, and he bade them quit the palace instantly.

On the following day at sunrise it became known to the people that both men had quit the palace where they had been staying. So the whole population ran to them, and they declared Hypatius emperor and prepared to lead him to the market place to assume the power. But the wife of Hypatius, Mary, a discreet woman, who had the greatest reputation for prudence, laid hold of her husband and would not let go, but cried out with loud lamentation and with entreaties to all her kinsmen that the people were leading him on the road to death. But since the throng overpowered her, she unwillingly released her husband, and he by no will of his own came to the Forum of Constantine, where they summoned him to the throne.

When Hypatius reached the hippodrome, he went up immediately to where the emperor is accustomed to take his place

*and seated himself on the royal throne from which the emperor
was accustomed to view the equestrian and athletic contests.*

*The emperor and his court were deliberating as to whether
it would be better for them if they remained or if they took to
flight in the ships. Empress Theodora spoke to the following
effect: 'My opinion then is that the present time, above all others,
is inopportune for flight, even though it bring safety. For one
who has been an emperor it is unendurable to be a fugitive. May
I never be separated from this purple, and may I not live that
day on which those who meet me shall not address me as mis-
tress. I approve a certain ancient saying that royalty is a good
burial-shroud.' When the queen had spoken thus, all were filled
with boldness, and, turning their thoughts towards resistance,
they began to consider how they might be able to defend themselves. All the hopes of the emperor were centred upon Belisarius
and Mundus, of whom the former, Belisarius, had recently
returned from the Persian war bringing with him an army which
was both powerful and imposing.*

*Belisarius, with difficulty and not without danger and great
exertion, made his way over ground covered by ruins and half-
burned buildings, and ascended to the stadium. Concluding that
he must go against the populace who had taken their stand in
the hippodrome – a vast multitude crowding each other in great
disorder – he drew his sword from its sheath and, commanding
the others to do likewise, with a shout he advanced upon them
at a run. But the populace, who were standing in a mass and not
in order, at the sight of armoured soldiers who had a great reputation for bravery and experience in war, and seeing that they
struck out with their swords unsparingly, beat a hasty retreat.*

*Mundus also made a sally into the hippodrome through the
entrance which they call the Gate of Death. Then indeed from
both sides the partisans of Hypatius were attacked and
destroyed. There perished among the populace on that day more
than thirty thousand. The soldiers killed both Hypatius and
Pompeius on the following day and their threw bodies into the
sea. This was the end of the insurrection in Byzantium.'*

Trajan's Column, Rome. Erected in AD 106 to commemorate the emperor Trajan's victorious campaigns in Dacia (modern-day Romania) and still standing today, this magnificent structure stands at 130 feet tall.

PART III
ROMAN TRIUMPHS

I

⸙ THE ROYAL TRIUMPH ⸙

F OR A ROMAN SOLDIER the Triumph was everything. To be
awarded a Triumph by the Senate of Rome in recognition of a
victory in the field was the very greatest honour a soldier could
hope to achieve. It assured him of fame, wealth and the admiration of his
fellow citizens. If he had political ambitions, it almost guaranteed him
the votes needed for high office. Above all, he rose to the semi-divine
status of being a triumphator, of supervising the sacred ceremonies of
victory at the Temple of Jupiter, the holiest spot in Rome. Ever afterwards, there was something majestic, almost divine about a triumphator.

For the Roman citizens the Triumph was the ultimate celebration of
their city, their state and their society. The ritualized parades and celebrations embodied what it meant to be Roman while emphasising the
power and grandeur of Rome. It was a time when the Gods came down
to Earth to celebrate the glory of Rome and her people.

Quite simply, there was nothing to equal the Triumph.

For a ceremony of such power and significance, information about
the Triumph is surprisingly obscure. The key religious duties of the triumphator were clear and rarely changed, but the format of the Triumph
could vary dramatically. And not only are some details unexplained, it
seems that even the Romans who carried them out did not fully understand their significance. We know, for instance, that the victorious general
had his face painted red for the Triumph, but not why. We know that the

crowd shouted obscene messages at the passing cavalcade, but their meaning is lost.

The Triumph was, in origin, a simple victory procession staged by the Roman army as it returned to its home city. Later writers recorded that the very first Triumph was celebrated in the 740s BC by Romulus, the first King of Rome. The City of Rome, then little more than a village with a few hundred inhabitants, fought against the nearby village of Caenina, a short distance to the northeast. Before the battle Romulus promised to dedicate his victory to Jupiter in his role as Feretrius, the Smiter of Enemies. Romulus killed Acron, King of Caenina, in single combat, and defeated the enemy. He then ordered the vanquished people to destroy their village and come to live in Rome, thus boosting the population of his own kingdom.

To fulfil his vow, Romulus then cut down an oak tree, a plant sacred to Jupiter, and carved it into a stand on which to hang the armour of Acron. This Romulus slung over his shoulder and carried back to Rome, followed by his men and by the citizens of Caenina. Romulus had on his head a laurel wreath to signify victory and his men sang songs. The procession marched up to the Capitoline Hill, where Romulus erected his trophy and offered thanks to Jupiter.

This first Triumph of Romulus was a relatively simple affair, and drew on Greek tradition for its format. The dedication of enemy armour, weapons or goods to the chief god of the victorious city was an established custom. The innovation made by Romulus was to make the procession by the returning army a part of this dedication ceremony. Indeed, the Romans made the procession the central feature of the Triumph, the dedication of trophies being an entirely secondary affair.

Romulus celebrated a second, similar triumph when he defeated the Antemanates, but his victory over the army of the powerful Etruscan city of Veii saw an innovation which lasted to Imperial times. The army of Veii had been led by an old general dressed in a purple cloak to show his seniority. In the Triumph this old man was led, dressed in chains, at the head of the group of prisoners. When the procession was over the unfortunate men were sent to the slave market. Thereafter it became traditional that the ceremony ending a Triumph saw a magistrate of Rome lead a grey-haired slave across the Forum and up the Capitoline

Hill. He then turned to face the Forum and shouted 'Etruscans for Sale'.

Numa, the second King of Rome, was too busy organising trade and religion to fight wars and so celebrated no Triumph. His successor, Tullus Hostilius was more aggressive, defeating the cities of Alba, Fidenae and the Sabines. The only detail of his Triumphs to have survived is the fact that King Mettius of Alba was dragged to Rome after the defeat of his city and executed. The fourth King, Ancus Marcius, fought only one war in which he defeated the Latins. He held a Triumph in which he and his men marched through the city to the Capitol, but the only detail recorded is that he dedicated more armour to Jupiter than any king before him.

When Ancus Marcius died, the throne was vacant. The Romans held an election and appointed Lucius Tarquinius Priscus, the son of an exiled Corinthian nobleman, as their king. Tarquin proved to be an able administrator and general, but he did like to make a good show and insisted that government officials should be accorded special dress and special privileges. As King, of course, Tarquin got more privileges and honour than anyone else. The city of Corinth was proverbial for its luxury and ostentatious wealth, so Tarquin was no doubt importing to Rome something of his home city.

One of his first actions was to begin building a temple to Jupiter on the Capitoline Hill. Tarquin could not believe that the chief god of the Romans was honoured simply by an oak tree, surrounded by trophies and a few statues. He began a Greek-style temple which was to feature prominently in future Triumphs.

One of Tarquin's innovations was to give each magistrate a servant known as a *lictor* to clear the way for him through the increasingly crowded streets of Rome. The servant was equipped with an axe to show the fate that awaited anyone who harmed his master. The axe was tied into a bundle of sticks which symbolized the people of Rome, showing that they were stronger when joined together. Together this object was the fasces, the symbol of Roman power. The most junior magistrates got one lictor, the higher ranks having more in attendance. As King, Tarquin gave himself twelve lictors.

Tarquin also gave himself and his officials a new form of transport, the chariot. As King, Tarquin had the largest and best. It was roomy enough to hold himself, a driver and a servant. The body of the chariot was embossed with mythological scenes and embellished with gold.

These innovations, and others, were brought together for Tarquin's Triumph, around 600 BC, Celebrated to mark the victory over the Latin city of Apiolae. When Tarquin held his Triumph he scorned the simple march past of returning soldiers which had suited earlier kings. He spent days preparing for his procession, supervising every detail with great care.

First in the procession came the senators, Tarquin wisely giving the more important citizens a role in things. They were followed by a troupe of trumpeters sounding out fanfares and flourishes. Next in the procession were prisoners taken from Apiolae and destined for the slave market. These were followed by a number of carts on which was piled the loot captured in the campaign. The Romans stared amazed at the wealth that was pouring into their city. They had never imagined that so much money could be taken in a military campaign. Behind the wagons marched the twelve lictors, symbolically clearing a path through the city to the emerging Temple of Jupiter on the Capitol. Next came Tarquin, dressed in a purple cloak and riding in his elaborate four-horse chariot of state. Behind him marched the army of Rome, the returning soldiers and officers who basked in the glory of the Triumph in front of their families and friends.

The great procession over, Tarquin took part in the traditional ceremonies on the Capitol. Then he unveiled another innovation as he led the population of Rome out into the Valley of Murcia to watch a series of games he had arranged. The site was later to be occupied by the great Circus Maximus, but at this point was an open valley.

As befitted a Greek, the games of Tarquin's Triumph were Greek athletics. In Greece, athletes competed completely nude to show the harmony and perfection of their bodies to the crowd as part of the worship of the gods. In Rome, public nudity was severely frowned upon. The athletes kept their underwear firmly on for the games. The Romans loved the horse racing and the spectacles, but the athletics were not very popular and soon fell out of favour. There was one exception: pugilatus, boxing.

The ancient sport of boxing had similarities to the modern sport, but in other ways was quite different. As today, blows were allowed only with the fist, so kicking, grappling or biting were illegal and could result in a boxer being disqualified. That apart, virtually any sort of punch was legal in Roman boxing, though there is a suspicion that later bouts banned punches below the chest. There were no rounds, nor did the fight have a set time limit. The fighting continued until one boxer was unconscious or gave up. Even if a man lay on the ground, his opponent could continue to punch him until a surrender was forthcoming.

Nor did the Romans separate their boxers into classes based on weight or size. Any fighter could expect to face any other in combat, the deciding factor being a draw of clay tablets from a pot at the beginning of the day's contests. In modern boxing, this would put a light man at a serious disadvantage. But in pugilatus there was no ring so a small man could not be pushed into a corner and pummelled into submission. Instead, a small boxer could run, duck and dive as much as he liked using the advantages of speed and space to tire a larger, more powerful opponent.

The traditional stance of a boxer was to stand in the same position as an archer. The left arm was held straight out towards the opponent with the palm of the hand facing forwards. From this position it would be possible to fend off the opponent or to push aside any punch coming forwards. The right arm was held close to the right chest, ready to launch a blow of great strength and violence.

The early boxers, such as those that fought in the games of Tarquin, wore leather straps around their hands. By about 400 BC this had developed into a sophisticated glove. The forearm was covered by a sheath of thick leather, lined with fur, which would absorb the impact of any incoming blows. The hand was encased in several layers of leather. The first joint of the fingers, which was the main point of impact when delivering a punch, was made more dangerous by a thick strap of tough, boiled leather with sharp edges. Inside the fist was held a D-shaped pad of leather to cushion the fingers when a blow was landed.

Injuries were common in this form of boxing. Broken noses, swollen eyes, dislodged teeth and split ears were numerous and brain injuries must have been more numerous then than now. Fatal injuries during boxing matches do not seem to have been particularly common, though they did occur. The real damage sustained from Roman boxing was in the long term as cumulative concussion had its effect on brain power.

After Tarquin's death his place was taken by an adoptive son, Servius Tullius. Born a Latin, Servius fought a series of wars against the Etruscans during which he celebrated three Triumphs in the same style as did Tarquin Priscus. Servius was murdered by his own son-in-law, a grandson of Lucius Tarquin Priscus known as Lucius Tarquinius Superbus, or Tarquin the Proud. This second Tarquin celebrated two Triumphs, but his main contribution to the development of the ceremony was to complete the Temple of Jupiter. The building was constructed in the Etruscan style and would afterwards be rebuilt more than once.

It was with the completion of this temple that the Triumph gained the setting for its climax. It was here that the sacrifices would be made and here that human blood would flow.

The Triumph of a victorious general makes its way through the streets of Rome during the late Republican era. The triumphator rides in a formal chariot pulled by white horses. Those soldiers who displayed great courage in the campaign march in front of the chariot, carrying the standards of the units that were engaged. The stone arch is the famous Triumphal Gate which marked the start of the triumphal route through the city.

II

' HAIL THE CONQUEROR '

I N 510 BC THE ROMANS OVERTHREW their last king, Tarquin the Proud, and established a Republic. The move was prompted when Tarquin's son raped the wife of a noble Roman, and the revolt was led by Lucius Junius Brutus. The ousting of the King left the Romans with the problem of how to organize their government. They decided to keep the power structure effectively as it was, but to open up the various government posts to election. In place of a king as head of the army and of government, the Romans invented the post of Consul. There were to be two Consuls elected annually to serve for one year.

The first real military victory for the new Republic came in 494 BC when the Consuls Appius Claudius and P. Servilius defeated the Volscian tribe and captured the town of Velitrae. Not unnaturally, the Consuls returned to Rome to celebrate a Triumph, as had the kings after a successful campaign. The other government officials were not sure that this was a good idea. They worried that the adulation bestowed on victorious generals might give Claudius and Servilius ideas above their station. Rome had just got rid of one king: it did not want two more.

The Roman Senate met to debate the problem. Already the Triumph was firmly rooted in Rome as an essential and much-loved festival of nationhood and victory. Moreover, the people enjoyed the procession and the accompanying games to such an extent that they might be seriously upset if the Triumph was denied to them. In the event, the Senate agreed to grant the victors of Velitrae a Triumph, with all the ceremonies, pomp and magnificence that had been enjoyed by the kings. They even added a new privilege. the triumphators would, for the rest of their lives, be given a special seat of honour at all the public festivals of Rome.

But the Senate imposed conditions, two of which proved crucial. First was the stipulation that in future only the Senate could award a Triumph to a successful commander. Before he celebrated a Triumph, the general had to come alone to the Senate and ask for a special tribute to be paid to the gods in recognition of victory. The Senate would then make its decision. Never again did the senators want to be put in the awkward position of having a victorious army at the gates demanding such a privilege. The second condition was that the triumphator had to have in the chariot with him a slave who whispered continuously in his ear a warning that he was not to be carried away by the adulation he received. We do not know exactly what the slave was instructed to say at this early date, but four centuries later his words were 'Remember that you are only human'.

Thereafter Rome fought for generations against its neighbours, the Samnites, the Volscians and above all the Etruscans and the city of Veii. In 396 BC Veii finally fell before the general Marcus Furius Camillus. Camillus was not Consul but Dictator, a position created by the Senate only in times of dire emergency and only for strictly limited periods of time. Camillus was awarded a Triumph for the capture of Veii, and was the first triumphator to hitch his ceremonial chariot to four pure white horses, a fashion followed by later Triumphs.

In 390 BC Camillus defeated the Gauls and was given a second Triumph. This time his innovation was to dedicate the spoils of war not to Jupiter the Smiter but to Jupiter Optimus Maximus – Jupiter the Greatest and the Best. The change was considered momentous in its day, though the significance is now lost. In 388 BC Camillus had a third triumph for defeating the Etruscans and in 385 BC an unprecedented fourth Triumph for crushing the Volscians. In 367 BC the 80-year-old was brought out of retirement to fight the Gauls again. Once more he was victorious and was given a fifth Triumph.

The Triumph was changing as the years passed. Gradually the triumphator acquired greater and greater prestige as if he alone and not the soldiers in the army had won the victory. In part this was a recognition that military skill and the favour of the gods was important, but it also reflected social changes in Rome as rich men became politically more influential and poor citizens less so.

In 338 BC a statue was erected to honour a triumphator for the first time. In 300 BC the Triumph first saw the victor dressed in a purple cloak embroidered with stars and a purple tunic decorated with palms. Soon afterwards the shields of the defeated enemy were nailed to the house of the victor for the first time. In 293 BC the bulk of the victorious army did not take part in the Triumph. Partly this was because armies were reaching such a size that to include them all in the procession would make the parade unwieldy, but it was also a reflection of the decreasing attention paid to the soldiers. Only those men who had been awarded medals or crowns for gallantry joined the Triumph. In 290 BC the glorification of the triumphator was further increased when his chariot was covered in gilding.

In 276 BC the first record was made of a feature that would become normal. It may already have been standard practice, but had simply not been written about. In that year the Samnites were defeated and their king and nobles were led through the streets in chains as part of the Triumph. When they reached the Temple of Jupiter the triumphator, Quintus Fabius Gurges, pulled the Samnite king from the parade and sliced off his head. The killing of the enemy king or leader was to become commonplace.

In 260 BC the Roman Consul Caius Duilius Nepos won a naval battle for the first time in Roman history. He was a given a Triumph, but the Romans had no idea how to celebrate a naval as opposed to a military victory. With no enemy shields or plunder to parade through the streets, Duilius sawed the rams off the front of the Carthaginian ships that he had captured. These were trundled through the streets in Triumph,then attached to a column in the Forum.

By 200 BC the religious aspect of the Triumph was formalized. The customs may have been much the same centuries earlier, but no records of this time survive. The triumph marched through the streets of Rome, pausing at each temple or altar it passed while priests came out to deck the temple with garlands of flowers.

Reaching the Temple of Jupiter, the triumphator was greeted by the priests with their togas arranged to cover their heads. The white oxen were led to the altar and had their throats slit so that their blood was caught in silver bowls. Together with bowls of wine these were given to the triumphator who poured them over the altar to honour the god.

At this moment, when the semi-divine triumphator stood face to face with the king of the gods, the human spoke to the god. He uttered a short poem:

> The enemy is defeated, the citizens are safe, the state is
>   tranquil, peace is assured.
> War has been brought to an end, the fighting is successfully
>   accomplished, the army and garrison are intact.
> Therefore, Jupiter, I give thanks to you and to all the other gods
> For the aid you have given me in taking revenge on my enemies.

In that moment god and human became one, Rome was united with her gods. It was a defining moment of great gravity and importance.

Once it was over, the games could begin.

Increasingly, the award of a Triumph became as much an act of politics as of military recognition. A man given a Triumph could reckon on scooping such prestige that he was almost bound to win any election he entered. The debates in the Senate about whether or not to grant a Triumph became heated. Quintus Minucius Rufus was refused a Triumph by the Senate on the grounds that the 'towns' he had claimed to capture were really 'villages'. Rufus was furious and led his army in parade outside the walls of Rome, watched by vast crowds.

The army became exasperated at the Senate more than once, so the soldiers devised their own method of giving due praise to a successful conqueror who was out of political favour at Rome. The soldiers would lift the general on their shields and hail him as 'Imperator'. It was the first appearance of a title which would later have such dramatic meaning in its developed form of 'Emperor'.

In 194 BC Titus Quinctius Flaminius returned to Rome after crushing the astonishingly rich King Philip of Macedon. He brought with him 43,000 pounds of silver, 14,500 gold coins, 3,714 pounds of gold bullion and hundreds of bronze or marble statues together with 1,200 released

Roman prisoners of war. The procession needed to display all this to the City of Rome was so vast that the Triumph took three days to pass through the streets. Rome had never seen anything like it, but she would see it again in the coming years.

The scale of the wealth pouring into Rome was emphasized by the triumphs over the eastern monarchies. When King Perseus of Macedon was defeated in 168 BC the share of the loot given to the Roman state was so enormous that all taxes were abolished for more than ten years. The sheer scale of treasure on display was breathtaking. So was the corruption that began to permeate the Roman political system. One triumphator was accused of cheating by taking some of the wealth rightfully belonging to the government. He escaped the charges of corruption by bribing the judges.

Victory followed victory, and Triumph followed Triumph. Carthage fell to Rome, so did Corinth, Athens and Sparta. There seemed to be no enemy that could defeat Rome, and Roman generals began to seek out wars. They looked on accidents as unforgivable insults and declared war when there was no real need to do so. What they wanted was a Triumph, for by celebrating a Triumph they could parade their glory and achievements before the voting public of Rome.

In 82 BC Lucius Cornelius Sulla returned from wars in the East and celebrated a Triumph of outstanding splendour. As well as what by now were the usual carts of gold, silver, ivory and statues, Sulla included several carts carrying the famous Library of Apellicon. Stolen from Athens for no reason other than that Sulla wanted it in his Triumph, the library included the original manuscripts written by Aristotle and the entire accumulated knowledge of the Athenian philosophers. After the Triumph, Sulla divided the books among his friends and colleagues and the collection was lost.

Like the first Tarquin before him, Sulla admired Greek culture. That year was one in which the Olympic Games were to be held. Sulla sent an army to Olympia and brought all the athletes to Rome so that the games were held there instead.

Sulla used the prestige of his victories and Triumph to engineer his appointment as Dictator of Rome. For some years the city had been wracked by political intrigues and riots as supporters of the conservative aristocrats fought against the more radical lower classes who supported peasant farmers and small businessmen. Before Sulla the political contest had been fought with bribery, rigged elections and riots. Sulla decided to bring peace to Rome by eliminating the leaders of the peasant party. Within a few days over 4,500 heads had been brought to Sulla's office so that the names of people on Sulla's list of death could be crossed off.

Following Sulla's example, ambitious young men in Rome took to organising Triumphs on the eve of elections. In 71 BC no fewer than four generals celebrated Triumphs for victories over minor opponents. the most successful of them was Gnaeus Pompeius, known as Pompey, who had been given his first Triumph for a war against Numidia in 81 BC. In 67 BC he quarrelled with a general named Metellus over who deserved the credit for defeating the pirates of Crete. The Senate gave the Triumph to Metellus, but Pompey ensured that the parade failed to feature any prisoners or loot so Metellus got little in the way of political credit.

Pompey then set off on a war against King Mithradates of Pontus, ruler of much of the Near East. By 64 BC the war was won and Rome had acquired large new territories. Pompey had acquired vast new wealth and an even greater reputation for military skills. Mithradates committed suicide rather than suffer the indignity of being led through Rome in a Triumph to help Pompey's ambitions.

Pompey still had enough for his Triumph. Held over two days in September 61 BC Pompey's Eastern Triumph was known for its sheer scale and bravado. No less than 300 kings, princes and governors were herded in front of Pompey's chariot. Pompey had signs attached to every cart to explain what it contained and where it had come from. At the front of the enormous procession a soldier carried a sign reading:

POMPEY THE GREAT, HAVING RESCUED THE SEA COAST FROM PIRATES AND RESTORED TO THE ROMAN PEOPLE CONTROL OF THE SEAS, NOW CELEBRATES A TRIUMPH OVER ASIA, PONTUS, ARMENIA, PHAPHLOGONIA, CAPPADOCIA, CILICIA, SYRIA, SCYTHIA, JUDAEA, ALBANIA, IBERIA, CRETE, BASTERNAE, MEDIA, COLCHIS, MESOPOTAMIA, PHOENICIA, PALESTINE AND ARABIA. AND HE HAS WON VICTORIES OVER KING MITHRADATES AND KING TIGRANES.

HAIL THE CONQUEROR

At intervals among the carts loaded with treasures were more signs, many of them displaying paintings of events which had taken place in the course of the long campaign. Pompey rode in a gilded chariot encrusted with precious stones and wore a cloak that had once belonged to Alexander the Great.

At the rear of the procession came a second great sign which proclaimed simply:

POMPEY THE GREAT CELEBRATES A TRIUMPH OVER THE WORLD

But even at the moment of his greatest glory, Pompey was aware of a young orator who was winning popularity by staging magnificent games, the man was Gaius Julius Caesar. The young Caesar was a gifted politician, but he was not wealthy. He looked for support to the relatives and friends of those executed by Sulla. In particular, his money came from Marcus Licinius Crassus, the richest man in Rome and a bitter enemy of Pompey.

Caesar gained for himself a great reputation for efficiency in the various posts he held in the Roman government, and was clearly a great speaker. But he lacked military achievements. In 58 BC he was given command of the province of Gaul, in reality only the Mediterranean coast and a small hinterland. Equipped with four regular legions and a large number of auxiliary troops, Caesar set out on a nine-year campaign of conquest which saw him overwhelm all of Gaul for Rome and even cross the sea to attack Britain.

Caesar sent regular public messages back to Rome giving updates on his conquests, always making certain to bolster his personal military skills. He won the undying loyalty of his troops by giving to them the rich spoils of victory, rather than sending them to Rome. In 48 BC the growing popularity of Caesar in Rome caused Pompey and his allies to prepare criminal proceedings against him which would begin as soon as he ceased being Governor of Gaul. Caesar responded by invading Italy and in a series of swift campaigns crushed Pompey and his aristocratic backers. King Pharnaces of Pontus, put on his throne by Pompey was dispatched. Pompey was murdered without Caesar's knowledge by Ptolemy, Pharaoh of Egypt, whom Caesar promptly defeated in turn. The final battle was in Africa against Pompey's ally King Juba of Mauretania.

Shrewd politician that he was, Caesar had not asked for Triumphs earlier, for he was confident that he could beat Pompey and the aristocrats with his army. But to gain supreme power in Rome itself, Caesar needed the support of the people. He had been saving up his Triumphs for that purpose and that alone.

In 46 BC Caesar held four magnificent Triumphs. The Triumph of Gaul, the Triumph of Asia, the Triumph of Egypt and the Triumph of Africa. Everything was carefully choreographed to reflect glory not just on Caesar, but also on Rome and on the citizens of Rome whose votes and support Caesar needed.

For the Triumph of Gaul, Caesar rode in a chariot of citron wood and followed a magnificent parade of wagons loaded with gold, silver and celebratory paintings. There were symbolic statues of the Rhine, the Rhone and Ocean, all bodies of water crossed by Caesar's armies. In the parade marched the Gallic leader Vercingetorix who had been kept in prison for six long years awaiting this moment. As the parade ended, Vercingetorix was strangled.

A few days later came the Triumph of Egypt. This time Caesar rode in a chariot decorated with tortoise shell behind a parade similarly decorated with wealth, arms, armour and paintings. One cart carried a model of the lighthouse at Pharos, complete with flames. In the parade marched the enchained Arsinoe, the beautiful younger sister of Ptolemy, who had died in the campaign. The crowd cheered, but they muttered when they saw the princess loaded down with chains. Caesar knew what he was doing, however. At the Temple, Caesar struck off the chains and sent Arsinoe into luxurious house arrest.

Next came the Asian Triumph, in which Caesar rode a chariot decorated with acanthus wood. It was in this Triumph that Caesar had a giant banner carried inscribed with possibly his most famous saying 'Veni, Vidi, Vici' – 'I came, I saw, I conquered'.

Finally came the Triumph of Africa with Caesar riding a chariot of ivory. Juba had been killed so his five-year-old son marched ahead of the chariot dressed as a king and loaded down with chains. Again Caesar spared the prisoner's life and sent him into comfortable imprisonment. Juba grew up to be a noted historian.

Caesar had had his Triumphs and had enjoyed them. He won the support of the people of Rome and overawed those he could not win over. These were the last great Triumphs of the Republic. Caesar's murder ushered in the civil war that led to his nephew becoming absolute ruler as the Emperor Augustus.

The Triumph was about the change again.

Bust of the emperor Augustus. By declaring that the Triumph celebrated the people, city and gods of Rome, Augustus made sure that he shared in the glory of his generals.

III

⟩ IMPERIAL EXCESS ⟨

THE CIVIL WARS which followed the assassination of Julius Caesar led to a profound change in the nature of the Triumph. The wars ended with the absolute victory of Caesar's nephew Octavian, known to history by his title Augustus. With his enemies defeated, Augustus set about reforming the Roman state and constitution.

He cleverly avoided taking the office of dictator or of flaunting his power openly. Instead he ensured that all the levers of patronage, wealth and influence were his alone. In this way he could usually ensure his favoured candidates won elections and that anyone who protested too loudly was banished. At the same time he maintained the fiction of democracy in Rome, thus avoiding the fate of his uncle who had been struck down by those opposed to dictatorial rule.

One of the most important ways of gaining adulation from the crowd was to win a military victory and stage a Triumph. From the first Augustus was subtly to alter the emphasis of the Triumph. No longer was the event held to celebrate the skills and prestige of the winning general, but to honour the power and might of Rome and her gods. As the most important citizen of Rome and supreme commander of the army who should take the lead role in the Triumph but Augustus himself? By proclaiming that a Triumph celebrated Rome and the gods, Augustus ensured that it could no longer be a vehicle for furthering the career of some politically ambitious general, but always enhanced his own glory.

The first Triumph of Augustus came while the civil wars were still continuing, but it set the pattern for much of what was to follow. Having defeated his enemies in Italy and Sicily, Augustus held a Triumph. The actual procession was relatively modest compared to the outrageous pomp of his uncle, but Augustus was clearly on his way to ultimate victory and the Senate and citizens of Rome fell over themselves to shower honours on the young man. The Senate gave him the permanent right to ride on horseback in the city and to wear a laurel wreath on all civic occasions, both usually temporary honours of great distinction. He was also voted a private seat in the front row for all state events and the honour of sitting with the Tribunes at Senate meetings. The priests of the Temple of Jupiter held a feast in his honour, then declared it to be an annual event.

As ever, Augustus was careful to give his generals a motive for fighting for victory. Although they could no longer play the coveted role of triumphator, the generals could look forward to being awarded the ornamenta triumphalia. The gold-embroidered purple clothes and gold medals that had once been the sole preserve of the triumphator, were now presented, on the recommendation of the Emperor, to the senior officers in a campaign. These men were sometimes allowed to ride in a carriage behind the chariot of Augustus.

One honour granted to Augustus in this first of his Triumphs was to have an arch erected over the route of the Triumph which was decorated with carvings of scenes of the campaign and inscriptions celebrating the deeds of Augustus. There had been earlier Triumphal arches of wood and canvas. The Arch of Augustus was of stone.

The fashion of building Triumphal Arches in stone was followed whenever the Senate wished to lavish particular honour. Among those to survive to the present day are the Arch of Titus, which celebrated his AD 81 victory over the Jews among others, and the Arch of Septimius Severus, erected in 203 to celebrate a victory in Parthia and Arabia.

As the number of stone arches proliferated in the early years of the Empire, the Triumphal Route became formalized. From its earliest days, the Triumph had passed through the Circus Maximus, where the largest number of spectators could be gathered, and had ended at the Temple of Jupiter on the Capitol for the final religious ceremonies. The precise route had, however, varied over the years. By AD 100, the route through the city had become fixed and remained unchanged over the coming centuries.

The great procession would muster north of the city itself in the open fields and wide suburban streets of the Campus Martius. It entered the city through the aptly named Triumphal Gate, heading south down the wide Via Lata before twisting west to pass through the Circus Flaminius. It then turned south again through a maze of narrow streets to emerge into the Forum Boarium, the old cattle market, and then went past the Altar of Hercules to traverse the vast open space of the Circus Maximus. The procession then headed northeast to pass in front of the Colosseum before heading northwest through more narrow streets to reach the Temple of Vesta and so enter the Roman Forum. The procession then continued along the Via Sacra, the Sacred Road used for religious processions, to the foot of the Capitol. Finally the Triumphator rode up to the Temple of Jupiter where he carried out his religious duties and executed the defeated king or general.

Not all enemy kings were executed. Subsequent emperors used Triumphs in their own particular ways. When the British King Caractacus was hauled through Rome in the British Triumph of the Emperor Claudius, it seemed his fate was sealed. He had fought an arduous ten-year campaign against the Roman invasion of Britain which had cost thousands of Roman lives and a vast sum of money. Dragged in chains to stand in front of the Emperor, Caractacus did not plead for his life. Instead he waved his arm at the vast array of marble temples and luxurious houses of Rome and asked 'If you have all this, why did you want my wooden home?' Lost for an answer, Claudius spared the Briton's life and put him into comfortable imprisonment.

Claudius' predecessor as Emperor, Caligula, had celebrated just one Triumph. His father, Germanicus, had celebrated a famous Triumph over the Germans some years earlier. Caligula therefore invaded Germany in AD 40, although there was peace at the time. The Germans melted away into the forests and no battle was fought. Caligula decided to invade Britain instead, but there were not enough ships to carry his army. He ordered the soldiers to gather sea shells from the shore and declared he had defeated the Ocean and stripped her of her wealth.

In August Caligula went back to Rome with a few German prisoners and his cartloads of shells. The Senate voted him a Triumph, terrified of his famously vicious temper if they refused. To ensure the mob cheered, Caligula had coins thrown into the crowd as he passed. Caligula's behaviour during and after the Triumph convinced his ministers and the Senate that he was totally deranged. He was murdered just four months later.

Between them Caligula and Claudius seriously devalued the importance and grandeur of the Triumph. Caligula by his bizarre behaviour and Claudius by handing out the ornamenta triumphalia to junior officers, not just to the commanding general of a campaign. The next Emperor took the Triumph to new heights of excess, luxury and ostentation.

Nero's first Triumph was celebrated for a fairly modest campaign against the Persians. It was a straightforward affair in which Nero played the role of triumphator and the victorious generals followed wearing their ornamenta triumphalia. Next came a Triumph over King Tiridates of Armenia. This victory was more in the way of a peace treaty than a conquest. After the procession Tiridates was given a diadem to wear and sat beside the Emperor to watch the festivities.

Nero was, in any case, not much interested in military matters. He was a poet and singer of talent who was fascinated by the arts and, in particular, by the culture of Greece. Nero decided on a completely new sort of campaign of victory, which would demand a new type of Triumph. Some decades earlier the athlete and musician Periodonicus had won more prizes at the Greek games than any other man. Nero set out to outdo Periodonicus.

In AD 66 Nero set out for Greece to take part in the Olympic, Nemean, Delphic and Corinthian Games, which had been specially delayed or brought forward so that they all took place that summer. Nero made it clear that he was going to take part in the competitions according to the rules. He would compete, he said, on a level playing field and would follow the rules scrupulously. Perhaps to the surprise of the organizers of the Games, Nero did exactly that. But the Greeks were under no illusions about this visit. The Emperor was coming to display his talents to them and expected to pick up a number of prizes in recognition of his skills.

Prominent athletes suddenly declared they were ill or turned up for events strangely out of condition. The judges at musical and dramatic contests knew what features of a performance to find most impressive, those in which Nero excelled. Even in contests where Nero had no real talent, the Greeks found something to praise and some excuse to award a prize.

A nasty moment came during the chariot race at the Olympic Games. Nero was only a mediocre driver, but the other competitors were wisely ensuring they kept behind Nero, but close enough to give the appearance of a real race. At the last bend Nero's chariot overturned. Short of pulling their horses to a sudden halt, there was nothing the other competitors could do except defeat the Emperor. The judges hurriedly conferred and then awarded Nero a medal for superb horsemanship in having righted his chariot and continued the race, even though he came last.

On his return to Rome, Nero celebrated a Triumph. The procession followed the traditional route and the people of Rome turned out in vast crowds to cheer their artistic Emperor. Instead of prisoners of war and booty, the triumphal procession paraded the palms of athletic victory and crowns of artistic merit which Nero had won. There were 1,808 in all to be carried through the streets. Nero did not march to the Temple of Jupiter, but to the Temple of Apollo the god of music. The Temple of Jupiter had, in any case, burned down a few years earlier and remained a charred ruin.

In AD 70 the Temple of Jupiter was rebuilt by the new emperor Vespasian. The temple was larger than its predecessor and was built entirely of marble, whereas the earlier structure had been of wood. Vespasian also set about restoring the Triumph. In AD 70 his son Titus crushed the Jews and secured large swathes of the Middle East for Rome. On his return Titus was given a Triumph jointly with his father.

The Triumph of 70 was consciously modelled on the great Triumphs of the past. The wagons were loaded with treasure stolen from Jerusalem, including the great seven-branched candelabra from the Temple. The traditional paintings of events in the campaign stood as tall as a three storey house and each was preceded by captives taken in the action portrayed. The Jewish leader Simon bar Gorias was flogged through the streets of Rome, then executed as the Triumphal procession ended. A stone arch was erected and this Arch of Titus still stands in Rome. It was only the first of the great Triumphs of Vespasian and his sons, Titus and Domitian.

After Domitian, the role of Emperor was taken by a succession of able men who each adopted their most promising subordinate to be their son and heir. Nerva, Trajan, Hadrian, Antoninus Pius and Marcus Aurelius ruled Rome for almost a century. They took the Roman Empire to its widest boundaries, conquering new provinces and re-establishing old ones. They reformed government and stamped out the worst forms of corruption. And they held Triumphs.

Trajan was a soldier Emperor who introduced a number of innovations to the Triumph, and greatly expanded the role of other features. His campaigns in Dacia in 102 and 106 gave him the opportunity to excel. The most enduring of Trajan's ideas was his erection of a record in stone of the campaign. Known now as Trajan's Column, the 800-foot long frieze winds up a 130-foot tall column and records in detail the feats of the army and Trajan's role in the campaign.

Trajan's second innovation was a restoration of an old practice. In the days before Augustus, Romans who gained a particularly noteworthy achievement were given an additional name by the Senate. In the case of victorious generals this was usually a form of the name of the country they had conquered. For instance, when Publius Cornelius Scipio defeated Hannibal in North Africa, the Senate changed his name to Publius Cornelius Scipio Africanus. Trajan revived the custom after his Dacian campaigns and had the Senate give him the name Dacicus. He went on to take the names Parthicus and Germanicus in honour of other victories which were given the status of Triumphs.

Finally, Trajan made a definitive link between the Triumph and the bloody spectacles in the arena. Previously the gladiatorial combats had been held only as *munera*, or a funeral ceremony to honour a dead relative. Trajan now included gladiatorial games in his Triumphal celebrations without the pretence of their forming part of a munera. The Dacian Triumph was followed by 123 days of events in the arena which saw 10,000 gladiators take part as well as thousands of animals.

After the extravagances of Trajan, neither Hadrian nor Antoninus Pius celebrated a Triumph. Both men spent their time reforming the Empire and establishing secure frontiers, leaving little time for the conquests and the Triumphs that went with them. In 166 Marcus Aurelius celebrated a truly magnificent Triumph over the Parthians.

But the splendour of the procession and the games that followed masked an unpleasant truth. Rome had won the war, but she had been on the defensive throughout the five-year conflict. The years of conquest were over. The years of defence were about to begin.

The Arch Of Constantine in Rome, built to commemorate Constantine the Great's victory over Maxentius, making Constantine the absolute monarch of the Roman Empire.

IV

, FALSE CONQUESTS ,

WHEN THE EMPEROR MARCUS AURELIUS died in March 180, he and his son Commodus were two years into a gruelling campaign against the German tribes north of the Danube frontier. Commodus' first action was to have himself proclaimed Emperor by his army. His second was to declare that the war was won and that he would celebrate a Triumph.

Leaving his subordinates to patch up a peace treaty with the barbarians, Commodus travelled back to Rome to hold his Triumph in October. All the trappings of a traditional Triumph were observed. Captive Germans were herded in the procession, captured weapons and looted treasures were displayed in carts and soldiers carried paintings representing the events of the war. Commodus painted his face crimson and donned purple robes embroidered with golden palms of victory before riding in his chariot along the usual route through the city. And, as usual, a slave stood beside him holding the laurel wreath of victory above his head and whispering 'Remember you are mortal.' More unusual was the fact that from time to time Commodus turned round to kiss the slave, his homosexual lover Saoterus. The Romans may have been impressed by the Triumph, but they were displeased by the open display of what most considered a vice.

Commodus himself, however, loved every minute of the celebrations, so much so that two years later he took advantage of a minor victory over the Picts in northern Britain to take the title Britannicus and hold another Triumph. This time there were neither prisoners nor booty on hand. Commodus rounded up some British slaves living in Rome and dressed them in Pictish costume to play the role of the conquered army in the procession. The following year, lacking even a minor victory to give an excuse for a Triumph, Commodus had himself proclaimed Emperor all over again and held celebratory games.

After the murder of Commodus by government officials fearful of his brutality, power fell to a career army officer named Septimius Severus. Disgusted by the empty Triumphs of Commodus, Severus determined not to hold any Triumph unless he had earned it. He was destined to celebrate the last great Triumph of Rome.

The war which gave Severus his chance for glory began in 195 when the mighty Parthian Empire attacked the Kingdom of Armenia, which was allied to Rome. For two years, Roman governors in the East held the Parthians at bay but in 197 Severus himself arrived at the head of a large army. Loading supplies and men on to a vast fleet of river transports, Severus led his forces down the Euphrates River deep into Parthian territory. The Parthian army was crushed and their capital city of Ctesiphon captured. The victorious Romans marched back up the Tigris River valley, taking with them over 100,000 slaves, together with the entire treasury of the Parthian Empire. Northern Parthia was made into the Roman province of Mesopotamia and Severus spent the following months reforming the eastern provinces.

In 200 the Emperor and his soldier son Caracalla returned to Rome to celebrate their great Triumph. It is unfortunate that few details of this Triumph have survived. Contemporary accounts are brief, stating only that it was the greatest Triumph in living memory and that it followed the traditional customs and patterns. The only firm fact known to us is that Severus was ill on the day and his place taken by his son Caracalla. The Triumph did leave one lasting monument. The massive triumphal Arch of Septimius Severus was built near the end of the Via Sacra where the procession paused before climbing up the slopes of the Capitol. It stands there still. Severus took the title Parthicus Maximus to celebrate his great victory.

Thereafter the Triumphs of Rome became increasingly empty affairs.

Caracalla, son of Severus, saw his armies win victories over the Germans, the Parthians and the Arabs and took the titles Germanicus, Parthicus and Arabicus in consequence. But he held no Triumphs for the victories were not great ones.

Later emperors were less fussy. In 231 Alexander Severus responded to an attack by the Persians, who had taken over the Parthian Empire, by again marching down the Euphrates and heading for Ctesiphon. The war ended in bloody stalemate with both sides having taken huge casualties and the frontier back where it had been before.

Despite this, Alexander sent a message back to Rome declaring that he had faced the entire Persian army in battle. Of 700 Persian war elephants, he boasted, 200 had been killed and 300 captured. Of 1,000 chariots, 200 were captured and vast numbers destroyed. In 233 Alexander entered Rome in Triumph. His chariot was pulled by four elephants in place of the traditional white horses.

After the murder of Alexander in a military coup, the Roman Empire fell into decades of chaos. In fifty years no less than twenty-five generals fought their way to the Imperial throne. None of them held power long enough to win a major war. Rome saw only one attempt at a Triumph. In 263 the Emperor Gallienus tried to boost such flagging support as he enjoyed by holding a Triumph in honour of some minor victories by his father, Valerian, and imaginary conquests of his own. Some tame elephants were dragged out to play the part of Persian war elephants and 1,200 gladiators dressed up as captured enemy soldiers. A group of actors was decked out in fur robes and long wigs to pretend to be Germans. Gallienus even erected a Triumphal Arch. The Romans drank the free wine and gobbled the free food, but they laughed at the supposed Triumph.

Ten years later the Emperor Aurelian defeated the rebel queen Zenobia of the eastern state of Palmyra and dragged her through the streets of Rome in chains. The Triumph was a good one by the standards of the day, but Aurelian wanted more. Having honourably won a Triumph over Palmyra, he took the empty titles of Germanicus, Gothicus, Sarmaticus, Armeniacus and Parthicus as well as the grand Restitutor Orbis (Restorer of the World) and the contradictory Pax Aeterna (Always Peaceful).

Stability was finally restored by Diocletian who took power in 284 and surprised everyone by reaching a compromise with his political opponents and refusing to execute his rivals. For the next 20 years, Diocletian fought numerous small wars on the frontiers and threw himself into the task of reforming the Empire. His administrative master stroke was to separate civil and military power in the provinces. No more would provincial governors have both the financial and military powers needed to stage rebellions.

In 303 Diocletian came to Rome to celebrate a Triumph for the first time. The Triumph was to mark victories in the many campaigns of his reign. He took names or titles for each of the campaigns, those designated Maximus alone numbering seventeen. Diocletian carefully carried out the traditional role of a triumphator and put on a good show of captured weapons, prisoners and loot. It was, however, little more than an act. Diocletian had not bothered to hold a Triumph in his twenty years of power because he did not need to. Power no longer resided in Rome, but wherever the army happened to be. It was the military which made Emperors and which held power in its armed hands. Diocletian held his Triumph of 303 because he was abdicating and wanted to end his reign with a traditional celebration.

Diocletian's abdication ushered in a fresh wave of military hardmen and coups which ended when Constantine the Great overthrew his rivals and became sole Emperor. A typical example of the way in which the Triumph was becoming debased is seen in the famous Arch of Constantine, which stands close to the Colosseum. In 312 Constantine won a civil war by defeating his rival Maxentius at the Battle of the Milvian Bridge almost at the gates of Rome. Determined to be seen to be on the winning side, the Senate hurriedly ordered the erection of this outwardly magnificent arch to celebrate the new Emperor's Triumph. The Arch of Constantine looks impressive enough, but it was thrown up quickly by tearing down earlier monuments and reusing the materials.

The Arch which supposedly celebrates a military victory of Constantine therefore includes a relief of Marcus Aurelius handing out food to the poor and another of Trajan speaking to his troops. Other panels show soldiers and barbarians dressed in fashions centuries out of date by the time of Constantine. The few pieces of sculpture made specifically for the Arch show signs of poor or hurried workmanship. Even in his moment of Triumph, Constantine could see the decline of Rome.

It was, perhaps, not surprising that Constantine abandoned Rome as the capital in favour of the more strategically situated city of Byzantium, which he renamed Constantinople.

And yet the ancient city of Rome remained the emotional heart of the Empire, and the mighty institution of the Triumph continued to exert a hold over the Emperors and the people. In 357 Constantius, son of Constantine, came to Rome to celebrate a Triumph after crushing a revolt in Gaul. There were no captives to lead in chains and no looted treasures to display in carts. Instead the Triumph took the form of a vast military parade as the entire mobile army of the Empire paraded through the streets along the traditional route.

Constantius took the classic pose of the triumphator with painted face and purple robes and rode in a chariot pulled by white horses. After the procession he supervised the celebratory games and spoke in the Senate. But there were two clear differences from earlier Triumphs. For the first time the Emperor made a point of being introduced to the senators and listening to the honours of their families. Earlier Emperors had not needed to do so as they lived in Rome and knew the senators well. More significantly for the institution of the Triumph, Constantius did not preside over the usual sacrifices and ceremonies at the Temple of Jupiter. Constantius was a Christian. When the procession ended, Constantius went off to a Christian church while the pagan priests and those senators who followed the old religion carried out the traditional ceremonies.

It was a defining moment. The first Triumph, held over a thousand years before, had been in essence a religious rite. Based on the Greek practice of dedicating trophies of victory to the gods, the Triumph had celebrated the mystical union of the city with her gods, of Romans with Jupiter. Although the parade and games had long been essential elements to the Triumph, it had been the core religious rites which had endowed the institution with its key dignity, importance and grandeur. Now that was gone.

The increasing importance of the new Christian religion to the Triumph was brought home to the people of Rome in 388 by the Emperor

Theodosius. Emperor in the East since 379, Theodosius came to Rome to hold a Triumph to celebrate assorted campaigns against rebel generals and the Goths.

The Triumphal procession followed the traditional forms and route. But, as Theodosius was a Christian the procession ended outside the precincts of the Temple of Jupiter. As those senators who were pagans made to enter the Temple to carry out the traditional sacrifice of white oxen, Theodosius ordered his soldiers to stop them. He told the senators that they had to choose between service to the pagan gods or to the Christian Emperor. After some embarrassed shuffling and an awkward silence the senators dispersed. Only the priests carried out the sacrifice.

In 403 another Emperor came to Rome to celebrate a Triumph. This time the triumphator was Honorius, son of Theodosius who had attended the Triumph of 388 as a child of ten. Honorius came to Rome claiming to have defeated that mighty barbarian king, Alaric the Goth. In truth the victory belonged to the general Stilicho. In any case the defeat was less impressive than it seemed for Alaric had brought only part of his forces to invade Italy.

The Triumph was celebrated in grand style. Honorius allowed Stilicho to ride in the triumphal chariot rather than to ride behind in a carriage. Both men were decked out with heavy gold jewellery, wore the traditional ornamenta triumphalia and had their faces painted. The soldiers of the Imperial Guard rode through the street wearing cloaks of scarlet silk and helmets topped by peacock feathers. The procession was followed by three days of celebrations with all the traditional Roman festivities of chariot racing, wild beast hunts and gladiatorial combats. It must have seemed like a return to the old days when Emperors celebrated real victories with Triumphs in Rome.

But it was an illusion. Just five years later Alaric the Goth stood outside the gates of Rome.

V

ꞏ BARBARIAN TRIUMPH ꞏ

F OR CENTURIES Rome had seen its kings, consuls and emperors march through the streets in Triumph after defeating foreign enemies. The wealth of the world had been looted and brought to Rome to be displayed in the Triumphs of the city's armies. But at one of the very first Triumphs held by Rome's first king twelve vultures had circled the city. A priest had predicted that this indicated twelve centuries of victorious Triumphs, after which only defeat would follow. By the year AD 400, 1150 of those 1200 years had passed by.

In October 408 Alaric, King of the Goths, stood outside Rome with his vast army of barbarians. The Roman Emperor Honorius was cooped up in the fortress city of Ravenna and his army was dispersed across the western provinces. Stilicho, commander in chief of the Roman Army had defeated Alaric five years earlier but now the only help he could send to the city of Rome was advice: 'Pay Alaric to go away'. The Senate of Rome emptied their treasury and gave the Goths 30,000 pounds of silver and 4,000 pounds of gold. Alaric marched away northward.

The failure of Stilicho to march to rescue Rome condemned him in the eyes of Honorius. Jealous courtiers fed the Emperor's suspicions and he ordered the execution of his general. With their beloved leader dead, the Roman army mutinied and fragmented. In 410 Alaric again marched on Rome. This time he was not to be bought off and laid siege to the city.

Somehow Alaric made contact with Gothic slaves inside Rome. He

Alaric, King of the Goths. In AD 410 Alaric, at the head of his Goth army, sacked the city of Rome itself, believed to be invulnerable since its founding twelve centuries earlier.

ordered them to gather together and attack the guards of the Salarian Gate in the chill hours before dawn of a night in August. On the appointed night, Alaric woke his army soon after midnight and led a small party of picked warriors to wait in hiding near the Salarian Gate. The slaves killed the guards and opened the gates, allowing Alaric and his men to pour in. A short, confused fight took place just inside the gate and several houses were burned. Then the Romans surrendered and Alaric gave his men three days to loot as much as they could take, then he set off south to escape the fast approaching forces of Honorius.

The sacking of Rome by Alaric was a cataclysmic event that shook the world. Nobody had really believed that Rome could fall to an enemy. The city had proved invincible for centuries and had acquired such an aura of majesty and power that it had seemed impossible that a disaster could actually occur. St Jerome, writing in North Africa, recorded 'Who could have believed that Rome, founded upon her triumphs which have blazed her name to the whole world, could fall to ruins? That she, the Mother of Nations, should also be their grave? That all the regions of the East, of Egypt, of Africa, should now be filled with swarms of young refugees from the former Lady of the World?'

It must have seemed that Rome had seen her last Triumph. That ultimate rite of Roman statehood and supremacy was gone. But this was not the case.

Just weeks after taking Rome, Alaric died. His Goths ordered a small army of Roman slaves to divert a river and dig a burial chamber in the riverbed. Alaric was laid to rest with the finest of the spoils of his victory. Then the dam was broken down and the river allowed to flow over him once more. To give added security to his burial place, the Goths then killed the slaves so that the site would remain secret. It has never been found.

Alaric was succeeded by his brother in law Athaulf and then by Wallia. These Goths chose to take Roman gold and grain in payment for their services rather than to fight against the crumbling, but still powerful Roman Empire. In 415 Wallia took his men to Spain and crushed a rebellion by the local Roman governor. Upon his return to Rome for his money, Wallia was given a Triumph by the Senate.

This Triumph of Wallia was an extraordinary affair. This was a barbarian king leading his barbarian army through the streets of Rome to the cheers of the Romans in the most important of all the Roman festivals. In theory the triumphator was the Emperor Honorius, but Wallia wore the ornamenta triumphalia and rode in the chariot alongside the Emperor. The warriors who marched in front of the chariot were Goths, and the prisoners led in chains were Romans. Yet most of the traditional elements of the Triumph were observed, though now there was no ceremony at the Temple of Jupiter at all.

The years that followed were chaotic as the Western Empire staggered under the repeated blows of barbarian invasion. No doubt Triumphs were held, but no record of them has survived. In 476 the last Emperor of Rome abdicated and the city became merely one more possession in the hands of barbarian kings. Yet the Triumph was not forgotten. The armies of the Eastern Empire still held Triumphs in the streets of Constantinople.

In 552 the Eastern Emperor Justinian sent an army to invade Italy and return Rome to the control of Romans. The army was led by Narses, an Armenian eunuch over seventy years of age. In a swift campaign of just two years Narses crushed the power of the Goths. In his victory speech, Narses compared the steadfast courage of his men to their Roman forefathers. This was odd as the army was made up almost entirely of Hun, Thracian and German mercenaries.

Then Narses went further and led his men to Rome to indulge in that most Roman of victory celebrations: the Triumph.

The centuries old customs were followed. The noblemen who claimed to be the Senate met Narses at the gates of Rome and escorted him to his triumphal chariot, pulled by four snow white horses. Wagons were loaded down with captured weapons and treasures, the prisoners were chained together and herded forwards by the jubilant victors. The old songs of victory were dug out and sung once again. The procession did not cover the entire route of the Imperial processions, but it ran through the Circus Maximus and up the Via Sacra to the Capitol Hill.

This was to be the last of the great Roman Triumphs. Not a single man in the procession was a true Roman, but they faithfully carried out the traditional roles developed so many centuries earlier by the victorious Romans. And they acted in the name of the Roman Emperor in

Constantinople. Just fourteen years later Rome fell to the barbarians again, this time finally.

But if the Triumph was dead, its influence and heritage were not. This had been the most important of all the Roman celebrations and it was to prove to be the most enduring.

Charles the Great, King of the Franks, better known as Charlemagne. In 800 Pope Leo III awarded him the title of 'Holy Roman Emperor'. He became defender of the faith throughout western Europe.

VI

⟩ INTO THE MODERN ⟩ WORLD

AFTER THE LAST ROMAN TRIUMPH which marched along the ancient route in the late summer of 554, no generals gave victory to Rome. But this did not mean the end of the Triumph. This greatest of all the Roman celebrations was so deeply ingrained in the Roman mind that even decades of defeat, starvation and humiliation could not remove it.

In 663 Constans II, Emperor of Constantinople, paid a state visit to Rome to discuss theological and political matters with Pope Vitalian. Eager to shower honours on his mighty visitor, Vitalian looked up the old records for guidance on how to welcome an Emperor to Rome. He came across descriptions of the Triumph and modelled the welcome given to Constans on these documents.

Where the triumphator had been met at the gates of the city by Senators, Constans was met by priests. Where the triumphator had been preceded by men and carts carrying banners and trophies proclaiming his victories, Constans was preceded by men and carts bearing crosses and banners proclaiming the victory of Christ. Mounted on a white horse, there being no chariot to hand, Constans was led in procession along the old triumphal route through the city. Near the ruined Circus Flaminius the procession left the old route to cross the Tiber and approach the Vatican. The procession ended at the steps of St Peter's. Some of the old traditions were abandoned. Nobody asked Constans to paint his face red, for instance.

Constans had won no great victory to justify the Triumph, the Pope had merely used the form of the Triumph to pay a great compliment to a visiting Emperor. It was a pattern that was kept to by the Popes in the following years whenever a foreign ruler visited Rome. With the Triumph resurrected in a new form, Rome began to revive other customs from the past. The Popes had already taken over one of the most coveted titles of old Rome. They styled themselves Pontifex Maximus, or Chief Priest of Rome. The title was of pagan origin and gave its holder the power to organize the calendar and to discipline priests who failed in their sacred duties. At first an elected office, it was later monopolized by the Emperors.

In the year 800 Pope Leo III resurrected an even more potent title, that of Emperor itself.

The man on whom Leo III bestowed the title was Charles the Great, King of the Franks, who is known to history as Charlemagne. Charlemagne ruled most of what is now France, Germany, Austria and northern Italy and was by far the most powerful monarch in western Europe. Leo needed Charlemagne's support against heretical doctrines, turbulent warlords and rival factions in the Church. His revival of the Imperial title was a carefully orchestrated act.

Ostensibly Charlemagne came to Rome in November 800 to settle a dispute within the Church. He was met outside the gates of Rome by the most magnificent triumphal procession anyone could remember. The form of the Triumph, as it was developed by the Popes was followed carefully. Charlemagne rode a white horse and was preceded by the crosses and banners of the Church.

The coronation took place inside St Peter's on Christmas Day. In placing a diadem on Charles' head, Leo used almost the same words as were used by the Senate when acknowledging a new Emperor. *Carolo piissimo agusto, a Deo coronato, magno pacifico Imperatori, Vita et Victoria*, intoned the Pope. 'To Charles the most pious Augustus, crowned by God, the great and peaceful Emperor, Life and Victory.' Only the reference to the Christian God in place of the pagan Jupiter showed that anything had changed.

After the coronation of Charlemagne the Popes adapted the Triumph to a new purpose, their own power and majesty. The occasion for the triumphal processions was now the coronation of the new Pope. Elements of the old rituals were incorporated into the papal coronation soon after the time of Charlemagne, but it was not until the coronation of Innocent III in 1198 that the full panoply was evolved.

Innocent III left his Lateran Palace riding a white horse decorated with red harness and trappings. The procession was the by now familiar one with priests and wagons carrying jewelled crosses and banners ahead of the Pope. The procession marched north to the Colosseum where it picked up the old Via Sacra of the original Triumphs, wound passed the mighty remains of the Roman Forum and ran around the Capitoline Hill. The route then left that of the ancient Triumphs to pass under arches of wood and greenery to cross the Tiber and reach St Peter's. Here Innocent was consecrated Bishop of Rome and Pontifex Maximus before returning along the triumphal route to the Lateran.

Meanwhile, the German Kings who followed Charlemagne kept the title of Emperor and many of them came to Rome to be welcomed with the triumphal procession. One Emperor, Frederick II who reigned from 1212 to 1250, took the Triumph more seriously than most. When Milan rebelled against his Imperial rule, Frederick swiftly defeated their army and captured the heavy battle cart decorated with sacred banners which had formed the emotional heart of the Milanese bid for freedom.

This *carroccio* was sent to Rome by Frederick in a solemn procession. It was dragged through the streets of Rome by his soldiers, past the ruined Circus Maximus and up the slopes of the Capitol to the crumbling Temple of Jupiter. There it was set on a marble plinth above an inscription which read 'Augustus Caesar Fredericus bids Rome to accept this carroccio as a tribute to the glory of their city. Captured during the defeat of the Milanese, it comes as a trophy in the Triumph of Caesar whose love for the city prompted him to send it, where it may be a witness to the disgrace of the enemy and the honour of Rome.' It was a triumphal trophy in the most ancient sense of the word. Romulus himself would have recognized the symbolism.

These German Emperors spread the idea of the Triumph across Europe. In 1443 King Alfonso I of Aragon celebrated victory over Naples with a triumphal procession. He rode in a chariot pulled by four white horses and was preceded by his troops in fine new uniforms. There were also carts in the procession, but instead of captured weapons and booty, Alfonso had them loaded with allegorical representations of virtue, fortune, power and other concepts. The triumphal chariot was never seen again, but the allegorical displays became favourite features of triumphal processions.

In 1536 the Emperor Charles V came to Rome to ride through the streets in Triumph after his victory over the French. Wooden arches were erected over his route, each painted with scenes of the campaigns and battles fought by Charles.

Gradually, however, nearly all the ancient elements were discarded. The sacrifice of the oxen did not survive the end of paganism. The painting of the face ended some time in the fifth century. The chariot was not seen after the Triumph of Alfonso of Aragon. But the Triumph did not end, it merely developed and changed. The Roman concept of celebrating a military victory with a parade followed by a religious service remains a potent and living tradition in the countries which once formed part of the Roman Empire.

In 1982 Britain and Argentina fought a war for control of the remote Falkland Islands. After the British had won the fighting, they commemorated their campaign by holding a grand military parade of the returning troops through the streets of their capital, followed by a religious service in their premier cathedral. The senior officers were given honours and decorations, while troops who had fought gallantly were given medals to wear in the parade.

It was a Triumph modelled on the ancient Roman original.

PART IV
BREAD & DEBAUCHERY

Teams of slaves hand out bread from the state granaries to citizens. The distribution of free food to the citizens of Rome was the basis of a vast government industry employing thousands of men as farmers, sailors, granary workers and bureaucrats.

I

˒ THE BREAD DOLE ˒

HUNGER AND FAMINE were ever present dangers in the ancient world. The chronicles are filled with accounts of hunger, famine and the mass deaths they caused. For today's readers, who need only visit the local shops to find an adequate range of foods on sale, it is difficult to appreciate fully the terror and familiarity of famine. We can even buy luxury fruits out of season after they have been flown in by jet aircraft from other countries. For the ancients there was no such supply system. If a crop failed, people starved.

Although the dwellers round the Mediterranean had access to a vast range of foods, they all relied for survival on a single staple crop: grain. Most villages and small towns depended almost exclusively on the grain fields in their immediate area for supply. In the vast majority of years these fields grew enough grain to feed the people, usually with a small surplus which could be charred and stored for the future. But if there was a wet summer or if crop disease struck, the food supply failed. Lacking a secondary staple crop, such as rice or potatoes – both of which were unknown in Europe at the time – there was no crop that could thrive in conditions fatal to grain.

The problem was especially bad in cities where large numbers of people were dependent on food imported from the surrounding countryside and were unable to fall back on wild plants or game in times of crisis. In AD 362 the entire area around the city of Antioch was struck by drought and the grain crops withered in the fields. Thousands of people starved to death as a result.

As Rome grew in size and population the problems famine could cause in the city became worse. By around 100 BC the city had a population of approximately a million people, which meant dragging in food supplies from not just the nearby fields but from farms hundreds of miles distant. It did not take much to disrupt the delicate food supply system and cause hunger, and famine was then close at hand.

It is no surprise, therefore, that the food supply was a major factor in Rome's internal politics and her relations with other states. When food shortages hit Rome there were a number of measures which the government could take. These seem to have begun to be implemented under the kings, but were not fully recorded until the later Republic. Among the permanent government staff who operated under the elected officials was a senior bureaucrat termed the Prefectus Annonae. His usual job was to inspect food imports for quality and to levy a tax, but in times of famine his role was crucial.

When a food shortage first struck, those who could leave Rome usually did so. Bulk grain could be costly and difficult to transport, so it was often easier to walk or ride a mule to a place were food was to be had. If the situation worsened the government provided transport for those people termed 'useless mouths', such as gladiators or domestic slaves, to be moved out of the city. Finally senators and government officials would be released from their duties and allowed to leave.

Meanwhile, the government had the power to requisition merchant ships. Forbidding the merchants to trade in their usual commodities, the Prefectus Annonae ordered them to sail to specified ports and return with grain. The Prefectus Annonae was empowered to set a price on grain to stop profiteering and to ensure that even the poorest could still afford basic foodstuffs. In extreme circumstances, he could take control of all private stocks of grain and ration food sales strictly. Such measures were usually enough to ensure that people did not die of starvation, but deaths on a large scale could occur.

Even when death was averted, the hunger could be very real. Politicians who promised to ensure adequate food supplies for the voting public were usually assured of a good hearing. By around 135 BC the food supply situation had become a major political issue. Vast estates run by slave labour had undercut the traditional peasant farmers of Italy and driven them out of business. This not only put the food supply into the hands of a few very rich men, with much potential for price-fixing, it also created vast numbers of unemployed citizens. These people drifted to Rome to live in abject poverty and work in what today would be termed sweatshops.

In 133 BC Tiberius Sempronius Gracchus and his brother Gaius formulated a programme of agrarian reform which limited the amount of land each man could own, gave impoverished citizens farming tools and capital to re-establish small holdings and radically reformed the food supply system for Rome itself. For over a decade the Gracchi, as the brothers were known, dominated Roman politics but first Tiberius and then Gaius was murdered by opponents and by 115 BC most of their reforms had been abolished.

The key surviving measure of the Gracchi Reforms was the dole. This system of grain distribution was designed to ensure that even the poorest Roman citizen would not starve. Large government granaries were built and the Prefectus Annonae charged with ensuring that they were always as full as possible. Once each month the granaries were opened. Each Roman citizen who queued up on the day would be sold a measure of about 30lbs of grain at a fixed price, usually about half the market price.

The Gracchi intended this as a temporary measure to alleviate urban poverty until their other reforms had taken hold and encouraged the urban poor back to a life on the land. When the other reforms were repealed, the dole became permanent. Those who received the cheap food were voters and would not willingly vote for anyone who removed their handouts.

In 90 BC the dictator Lucius Cornelius Sulla abolished the dole. Having come to power as the leader of the aristocratic faction in government, and been maintained there by the swords of his soldiers, Sulla had little need for the votes of the 50,000 poor citizens who queued up monthly to get their cheap grain. After his death, however, the dole was quickly restored. In 58 BC the rabble-rousing demagogue Publius Clodius was swept to office after promising in the election to make the grain dole free of charge.

The monthly supply of free grain led to a huge growth in the number of people applying for the dole. By 44 BC no fewer than 320,000 men were getting their free measure of grain every month. In that year Julius Caesar, then at the height of his powers, ordered a crackdown. Inspectors stood at the granaries and only those adult men who could prove they were Roman citizens were given the grain. The number of recipients fell dramatically to just 150,000.

The lure of free food proved to be incredibly attractive. The population of Rome increased steadily as any citizens who fell on hard times moved to the city to take advantage of the grain ration. This system had a slow, but profound effect on society across the Roman Empire. In cities as diverse as Antioch, Alexandria and London there came to be a clear socio-economic divide between citizens and non-citizens. The Roman citizens all tended to be fairly wealthy and independent because, if they weren't, they moved to Rome. Although some non-citizens might be wealthy the vast majority were poor or middle class. The tensions this created became increasingly obvious in later centuries.

The effects on the society in Rome itself were equally marked. The increasing influx of poor citizens, all of whom had the vote, increased the potential for bribery in elections. Already corrupt, the government of Rome became notorious for the greed and immoral nature of its elections and day to day conduct. Eventually political power was effectively concentrated in the hands of a single man, the Emperor, who had the control of the dole, the public games and other methods of patronage.

Rome, meanwhile, was becoming a burden on the Empire. The effects of this were slow to develop, but proved nonetheless severe. In the early years, Rome had supplied soldiers for the army, administrators for the government and wealth to drive the enormously powerful state. By the time of Caesar it was a magnificent city of marble temples and public buildings, the seat of government and the basis of power.

Gradually, Rome became merely an empty if glorious shell. The population became mere consumers of food and wealth, creating little and contributing less to the Empire. While the votes of the citizens and the voice of the mob still controlled power, Rome remained pre-eminent. But slowly the final arbiter of power became the army. And the army was increasingly manned and run by men who were not from Rome.

At the time of Augustus, however, such developments were so far in the future as to seem impossible. In AD 10 Augustus introduced a means test on the dole in an attempt to reduce abuses of the system. The number of recipients stabilized at around 200,000, where it remained for the next 300 years.

The dole was handed out in the form of grain as this was the form in which it was stored by the state and, thus, was most convenient for those measuring it out. For the recipients, however, the grain was not terribly convenient.

The majority of poor people in Rome lived in tenements several storeys high, often an entire family sharing a single room. Such homes had no running water and no fireplaces. Water was obtained from a nearby fountain, supplied from rural springs via aqueducts, and often stored in a barrel in the room. Heating for cooking came from squat iron braziers burning wood or charcoal. On these braziers pots could be boiled or food grilled. The opportunities for cooking grain in such circumstances were limited.

The basic method for preparing grain in such a home was to pound it in a mortar to produce a consistency not unlike modern porridge oats. This could be boiled with water or milk to form a thick gruel, or used as a base for hearty dishes. One recipe from about AD 50 is for a thick vegetable stew and reads:

> Soak dried lentils and peas. Crush grain and boil in water with the dried vegetables. When it is cooked, add some olive oil. Chop some greens, such as leeks, coriander, dill, fennel, beet or cabbage. Put these chopped greens into the pan. Boil further. Pour this mixture into bowls and serve with freshly chopped cabbage leaves on top.

Another recipe was aimed at those who could afford some meat:

> For a hot savoury stew of kid or lamb. Chop the meat into pieces and place in a pan. Chop an onion and some coriander, and pound together pepper and cumin in olive oil. Add to the pan. Boil in wine. When it is cooked thicken with pounded grain. Turn into a shallow dish to serve.

Such dishes were nutritious, but most Romans preferred to eat bread. Turning grain into bread involved first grinding it into flour then baking it. Neither milling stones nor ovens were standard equipment in poor homes, so those on the dole often took their grain to bakers. They could either pay for the grain to be turned into bread, or the baker might take a proportion of the grain in lieu.

Roman bread came in a wide variety of shapes, sizes and types. The most highly prized was white, wheat bread baked from flour carefully sifted after just one milling. Wealthy people ate little else, using the bread in a wide variety of cooked dishes as well as serving it as bread. The less well-off could buy bread made from a less fine sieving which was rather darker, but could be improved in colour by adding a small quantity of chalk.

Most people, however, ate what was termed 'army bread' as it formed the basic ration for serving soldiers. This bread was made with wholemeal wheat flour, no other grains being added, ground fairly coarsely. It was made into a yeast dough with olive oil, water and salt, sometimes with herbs added for flavour. The dough was shaped into rounds about eight inches in diameter and marked across the top into segments. When baked, the bread rose to be about two inches thick.

The really poor were in the habit of swapping their dole of wheat grain, or at least part of it, for rye grain. Rye was darker, had a less favoured taste and was more susceptible to mould or fungus, some of them deadly. As a result wheat grain could be swapped for a larger quantity of rye, providing more food. Rye produced a dark bread which, although nutritious, was not much liked by Romans.

Whatever sort of bread a family might have, they were unlikely to waste it. There are numerous recipes for using up stale bread in stews or soups. One simple dessert was made as follows:

Take old bread and break into large pieces. Soak in milk. Fry in olive oil. Pour honey over bread and serve.

The problems of what to do with the grain were solved by the Emperor Aurelian in about 270. He organized a thorough reform of the dole system. Aurelian was a professional soldier created Emperor by the army, and one of the most formidable administrators ever to rule Rome. Perhaps frustrated by the lack of military discipline in such an expensive area of state activity as the dole, Aurelian set about making it more efficient.

In an effort to halt hoarding of grain and its resale for cash, Aurelian replaced a monthly grain distribution with a daily bread dole. Each citizen who presented himself for the dole received six of the round, flat loaves of 'army bread'. On holidays jugs of wine were also doled out along with olive oil and pork. Such a daily dole was more than was needed by a single man, but most citizens had families.

The reforms of Aurelian called for the baking every day of around 1.2 million loaves of bread. This huge undertaking was entrusted to an army of bakers working virtually round the clock in the Imperial bakeries. The leading craftsmen were citizens or freemen employed by the Emperor on long term contracts. Later the contracts were made permanent and strict penalties were enforced on anyone who sought to leave the job unless he provided a replacement to take over his work. The bulk of the workforce was, as usual in Imperial businesses, slaves.

The circular kitchens of the vast Imperial bakeries had walls studded with cavernous, domed ovens made of thick clay. In the evenings large wood fires were lit in the ovens and fed continuously for some hours. When the oven walls were hot enough, the glowing embers were raked out and removed. The dough was then pushed into the ovens to cook with the heat stored in the clay walls.

The huge quantities of first grain and later bread being handed out free in Rome were but a fraction of the total amount consumed by the city. Grain equivalent to something over seven million loaves was eaten each day in Rome. The fields of central Italy were quite unable to supply such a large demand, so the Romans looked abroad for their supplies.

1. *Corazza Imperiale, nell'arco di Costantino*. 2. *Corazza a maglia, ed Elmo, che portavano i Soldati Romani, nell'arco di Costantino*. 3. *Lancia romana a bassoriliero nel Castillo Barriationi*.

Roman armour, discovered beneath the Arch of Constantine in Rome. As Rome expanded in the third and second centuries BC, the army was increasingly called on to secure new areas of food production for a hungry Roman populace. The fertile island of Sicily, lying as it did within a few days' sail of Rome, was an obvious place to start.

II
˒ WAR IN SICILY ˒

THE AWESOME DEMANDS of the mighty city of Rome for food, both basic and luxury, were a driving force in the internal politics of the state. Private fortunes and political careers could be won or lost on the issue of food. The threat of famine could provoke maddened mobs literally to tear officials to pieces. It was hardly surprising that the need to keep the great city supplied with food was so often the deciding factor in Rome's international relations.

As Rome increased her population and expanded her power across Italy in the fourth and third centuries BC, she found herself increasingly in need of a reliable supply of food. The farmlands of central Italy were not fertile enough to feed Rome's growing population and increasingly large army. Nor was the climate ideal for large scale production of wheat, the staple food of the Romans. The shortfall was made up by buying in foods, particularly grain, from elsewhere. More and more often that meant from Sicily.

This astonishingly fertile island was producing far more food than its population needed and exported the surplus in large quantities. The chief export was the grain needed by hungry Rome. So much grain was grown on Sicily that the island took Ceres, goddess of harvested grain, as its patron. The worship of the goddess was surrounded by mystery and secrets. Her temples were usually built in remote rural areas, not in cities, and were staffed by priests sworn to total secrecy about the rites and duties they performed.

Roman writers portrayed the goddess as presiding over drunken orgies at her temples in Sicily. They may have been confusing her with the sex goddess Aphrodite. The temple of Aphrodite at Eryx, in north-western Sicily, maintained a number of priestesses who worshipped the goddess by engaging in sex with her male devotees.

Nor was Sicily famous only for her grain. The hillier regions were home to immense flocks of sheep. So many sheep ran over the hills that Greek poets habitually termed the island 'Sicily of many sheep'. The wool from these flocks was exported in great quantity as was cheese made from their milk. Cheese from cow's milk was another export, the herds being kept on grasslands beside the rivers, which flooded too often for the meadows to be ploughed.

Sicilian honey had a magnificent reputation. The richest Romans prided themselves on serving honey from the proverbially floral slopes of Mount Hybla. The olives were equally valued, usually in the form of *epityrum*, a preserve made by chopping black olives finely and mixing them with vinegar, coriander, cumin and mint before packing them tightly in jars and covering them with olive oil. Sicilian grapes were dried into sultanas and currants for export.

It can be little wonder that the Romans looked upon Sicily as a land of luxurious plenty. Given the Roman habit of invading places, it was perhaps only a matter of time before they turned on this politically frag-mented island.

Rome's chance came in 264 BC. The Sicilian city of Messina had been at war with its larger neighbour Syracuse and had enlisted help from the North African city of Carthage. Carthaginian influence was strong in western Sicily, where there were a number of Carthaginian colonies and trading posts. When the war ended in victory for Messina, the Carthaginians asked for the share of the booty they had been promised. The Messinians, however, found a pretext to avoid paying and called on Rome for help. It was the start of a conflict that would not end for more than a century.

The war opened with the Romans sending an army to Messina and marching down the east Sicilian coast to conquer the area with most pro-ductive grainfields. The Romans had a small fleet of twenty triremes, vessels with three banks of twenty-eight oars with one man to each oar.

They were hopelessly outclassed by the 200 prowling Carthaginian ships, most of which mounted five banks of rowers. These quinquereme ships did not have five banks of oars, but two banks of thirty oars rowed by five banks of oarsmen, three men on the upper oar and two on the lower. This arrangement made for a wider ship and much greater speed than could be achieved by the trireme.

The Romans called on Greek assistance and, with a wrecked Carthaginian warship as a guide, produced a fleet about 100 ships strong. Although modelled on the Carthaginian quinqueremes, the Roman ships had a secret weapon in the shape of the *corvus*. This was a swivelling gangway which could be hoisted up on a gantry and then dropped on to an enemy ship. A metal spike at the far end of the corvus gripped the opposing vessel, stopping it from backing away. Meanwhile a large force of Roman troops poured over the gangway to board and capture the enemy.

The Roman fleet encountered 130 Carthaginian ships off Mylae in northern Sicily in 260 BC. The Roman corvus took the Carthaginians entirely by surprise and they lost fifty ships before they could disengage. Now confident at naval warfare, the Romans launched an invasion of Carthaginian territory in North Africa, sending a large army in transport ships accompanied by 330 warships. The fleet was met by 350 Carthaginian warships off Cape Ecnomus in southern Sicily. The Romans again won, but their invasion was defeated on land. The returning fleet was wrecked by a storm not far from Cape Ecnomus, losing 284 ships and 50,000 men.

The land war on Sicily had, meanwhile, been continuing and by 249 BC the Carthaginians had lost control of all the productive farmland and were trapped in their main base of Lilybaeum. The fortress was virtually impregnable and could not be starved into surrender as fast Carthaginian supply ships evaded the blockading Roman fleet. Hearing that the main Carthaginian fleet was nearby off Drepanum, the Roman commander, Claudius Pulcher, decided on a surprise attack to make a final break of the enemy supply lines. Before setting off to attack, Claudius Pulcher followed Roman custom and asked his priests to consult the prophetic chickens. The priests had first to feed a sacred meal to the chickens before sacrificing them and inspecting the entrails. Pulcher and his commanders gathered for the ceremony, but the priests were deeply worried. 'The chickens will not eat,' they told Pulcher. 'Then let them drink', the general replied, and hurled the birds into the sea.

The Roman omens were not good, but it was the superior planning of the Carthaginian Admiral Adherbal which won the day. In all ninety-three Roman ships were lost and just thirty escaped the disaster. A few weeks later a replacement Roman fleet was wrecked in a storm.

The decisive battle of the war came in 242 BC when Lilybaeum was again put under siege by Rome. This time the Roman blockade was more effective and Carthage had to send a fleet of some 200 ships loaded down with supplies to break through. The fleet was met off the tiny island of Hiera by a Roman fleet of about equal strength under the command of Lutatius Catulus. Unhampered by heavy stores, the Roman ships proved to be more manoeuvrable and won an easy victory, only fifty Carthaginian ships escaping the disaster.

Finding himself starved of supplies and with no hope of relief Hamilcar, the Carthaginian commander on Sicily, had little choice but to surrender. Formal peace was made in 241 BC. The various city states and kingdoms of Sicily were reorganized into a Roman province. Roman taxes were imposed and Roman merchants came to buy the rich agricultural produce of the island.

Rome looked forward to days of plenty and set out to enjoy them.

III

ꞏ BANQUETS OF ꞏ DEBAUCHERY

THE SCALE AND DEBAUCHERY of Roman banquets and orgies has become legendary, with their roast lark's tongues and braised giraffe necks marinaded in honey – and the sexual excesses.

But it was not always so. The early Romans prided themselves on self-reliance, modesty and frugality. The change came slowly, after the Roman conquest of Sicily in 241 BC. For the first time the Romans tasted the luxurious foods that other peoples had known for centuries. The rich culture and diet of Sicily gave the Romans a hint of what they had been missing. As conquest followed conquest, Romans acquired both the access to exotic foods and the wealth to buy them. By 75 BC Rome was producing cookbooks on how to enjoy these new foods and drinks. A century later the Romans were indulging their tastes to the full.

The first emperor to become notorious for the debauchery of his dinners was Caligula. Caligula came to power in AD 37 at the age of twenty-four. His reign began well, but he then became seriously ill and fell into a coma. When he recovered Caligula was a changed man, many thought he was mad. He took his sister Drusilla as wife, and when she died picked up a notoriously depraved prostitute named Caesonia. Caligula used his guards to assasinate anyone who displeased him, or sent men to trial in front of bribed judges to be whipped, stripped of their property or executed.

If he tired of Caesonia, Caligula would invite couples to dinner. The

Romans Of The Decadence, a picture by Couture which hangs in the Louvre in Paris, shows a late Roman banquet in full swing.

man would be left outside while the wives were brought in to enjoy an intimate time with the emperor. Sometimes Caligula was interested only in conversation, but he could force himself on the women with the threat of having their husbands executed if they refused. When Caligula next met the husband, he often engaged him in lighthearted banter on the subject of his wife's beauty and performance in bed.

The emperor's whims were notorious, and men invited to dine were never entirely certain how the meal would go. A favourite stunt of Caligula's was to have the senators stripped of their togas and dressed as slaves, then forced to serve at table. He was also fond of instructing his staff to cook up bizarre and disgusting dishes, then forcing his guests to eat them. On other occasions Caligula dressed as a woman for the dinner, or as a god. At one such dinner, Caligula suddenly broke off his conversation to chat to the god Jupiter who he claimed had entered the room. 'You can see him, can't you?' Caligula demanded of a guest. 'Only you gods, my lord, can behold each other,' replied the man. Caligula laughed.

More grim was the event in AD 40 when he invited the two Consuls, the most important officials of Rome, to dinner. In the middle of eating, Caligula suddenly collapsed in laughter, almost choking on his food. 'What is it?' asked the Consuls. 'Oh, nothing,' Caligula replied. 'But I just had the thought that I could have both your throats slit as you dine.'

Such threats were not empty. Dining at the Imperial table became a dangerous occupation. Caligula was losing his hair and was very touchy on the subject. More than once he had men with good heads of hair arrested and shaved. When one young man unwisely turned up to a banquet with his beautiful hair freshly washed, doused with perfume and sprinkled with gold dust, Caligula had him murdered. Such a man was too dangerous to have as emperor. In January AD 41 Caligula was assasinated.

The emperors that followed Caligula were more restrained in their violence, but not in their other habits. Nor were their wives. Messalina, wife of the Emperor Claudius, is said to have created a state within a state – a 'pornocracy' – in which her lovers were accorded high office and her enemies killed. The satirist Juvenal and the letter-writer Pliny the Younger both recount extravagant tales of her activities, including her attendance at brothels where she would service the customers as a prostitute herself.

She once worked her way through the entire crew of a warship that had just put in to harbour. Claudius eventually had her executed, not for her sexual exploits but for being implicated in a plot against him.

However none of the emperors could outmatch Elagabalus, who came to power in AD 218. Aged just fourteen when became emperor, Elagabalus inherited the Empire from his uncle Caracalla. The boy's real name was Varius Avitus Bassianus, but he was known as Elagabalus as he was the hereditary high priest of that Syrian sun god. Arriving in Rome, Elagabalus ordered the construction of a temple to his god on the Palatine Hill. He then got down to the serious business of debauchery.

The new emperor loved banquets, the giving of which quickly became one of his favourite pastimes. He had a special chamber built in the Imperial palace so that he could invite more guests than earlier emperors had been able to do and fitted it with some very unusual features.

The entrance to the room was made especially wide, for Elagabalus liked to make a spectacular arrival in front of his guests. Sometimes he danced in followed by a troupe of musicians, on other occasions he entered in fancy dress and challenged the guests to say who he was pretending to be. More ostentatious was the golden chariot which the young emperor would have hitched to a variety of animals for a dashing debut. He would enter pulled by tame lions, crocodiles, an elephant or bulls. He once tried harnessing a rhinoceros, but the animal did so much damage that even Elagabalus decided not to use such an animal again. His favourite entrance, however, was to ride the chariot while completely naked except for a garland of roses, and pulled by four equally unclothed young women.

The room also had a false ceiling that could be slid to one side in seconds by a team of slaves on the floor above. Elagabalus filled the false ceiling with flowers, then had it pulled aside to create a blizzard of blossom to fall on his dinner guests. Once he overdid it and a guest suffocated in violets.

In the next door room, Elagabalus had a swimming pool constructed. For banquets this was filled with water scented with costly perfumes. In between courses he stripped off and splashed about to wash himself. Favoured guests were invited to join him.

Nor did Elagabalus stint on the foods served up at his entertainments.

At one feast he served up 600 storks, first eating the tiny brains himself with a golden pin before the birds were served to the guests. One day in midsummer he surprised everyone by having a cart load of snow trundled into the room. The snow had been brought from the high Alps on a convoy of wagons, wrapped in straw to stop it melting.

Practical jokes were frequent. He had a wide variety of false foods to hand, made from wood, ivory, wax and pottery. These were slipped on to dishes and served up as if real, the emperor roaring with laughter when a guest tried to eat a fake delicacy. Pies were served up that,when cut, were found to be filled with live frogs, snakes, cockroaches or scorpions. The emperor enjoyed the jokes hugely.

Elagabalus had a sexual appetite as vast as that for jokes and food. Every banquet he held had a number of prostitutes, both male and female, to hand. The emperor made no secret of what he was up to if he slipped out of the room with one or two of them for a while. His guests were, of course, free to indulge themselves as well. Elagabalus would dress as a woman when he was after male prostitutes, and officials across the empire were under orders to send to Rome any male slave they came across with especially large genitalia. At one point Elagabalus gave up women altogether and 'married' a man named Hierocles. The 'marriage' did not last long and soon the emperor was back with the women.

By the summer of 221 it was obvious that Elagabalus was not only a debauched drunk, but also a bad ruler who would not allow talented officials to do their jobs without interference. The Senate and his family brought in the emperor's infinitely more sensible cousin Alexander Severus to be joint ruler in the hope of getting some sense into the administration. The only result, however, was that Elagabalus became jealous of his cousin and convinced himself that a coup was being plotted. He ordered the Praetorian Guard to kill Alexander, but the tough soldiers had had enough of the effete young drunk. They killed Elagabalus instead.

Elagabalus took everything to extremes, but opulence was not restricted to the emperors. The first Roman to achieve fame for the luxury of his parties was Marcus Gabius Apicius, who died around 50 BC. A Roman nobleman who became stupendously wealthy through land deals and slave farms, Apicius entertained the most cultured men and women of Rome and maintained a number of cooks famous for their skills and the variety of the meals they could produce.

Rather better known was his descendant, another Marcus Gabius Apicius who was born about AD 5. Traditionally this Apicius was thought to have written the famous cook book *De Re Coquinaria*, or *The Art of Cooking*. It is now considered more likely that the book was written by a professional cook and merely dedicated to Apicius. Whoever wrote it, the book provides an insight to the sorts of dishes which graced the tables of upper class Romans of the period.

Some of the recipes are vague as to quantities, and a few contain ingredients with names that cannot be understood. On the whole, though, the cook book of Apicius shows a gourmet interested in fine ingredients and well-balanced dishes. There is a plentiful use of vegetables, fish and poultry, though beef and pork feature as well. It seems that it was the lavish use of oriental spices, such as pepper or saffron, that gave Apicius his reputation for extravagant entertainment. Such ingredients are commonplace today, but were rare and enormously expensive in ancient Rome.

One recipe for 'Chicken in the Numidian Style' runs as follows:

Pluck, clean and boil the chicken, sprinkle it with asafoetida and pepper, then roast. You grind pepper, cumin, coriander seed, root of asafoetida, date wine and nuts. Add to this vinegar, honey and oil. Boil it well, then bind it with flour and pour over chicken, sprinkle with pepper and serve.

The liberal use of spices is clear, but less obvious to modern eyes is the sheer luxury of roasting the chicken. Wood-fired ovens were expensive to build and needed constant attention if they were to perform well. The casual acceptance that the cook will have an oven to hand, together with a slave to operate it, shows the book was intended for wealthy men only.

By contrast the recipe for cooking a joint of bacon is simplicity itself. 'Cover it with water and boil it with a lot of dill. Add some drops of oil and a little bit of salt. Serve'

Cooking the meal was, however, only a small part of the effort needed to throw a truly successful dinner party in ancient Rome. Given the dreadful state of the drains in the city, having a pleasant smell in the dining area, or *triclinium*, was essential. Vases of flowers and dishes of aromatic leaves were placed about the room, but most guests expected to be presented on arrival with a wreath of flowers to wear during the meal. Perfume was also sometimes handed round for guests to use: it was considered an insult for a guest to bring his own, as this implied the host's house stank.

The wealthier the host, the more exotic the fragrances. A relatively humble man would opt for flowers grown on the nearby Sabine Hills. A nobleman would use roses brought by galloper from Campania, a region famous for its blooms. Cheaper perfumes were made from rose water, but the aristocracy used balsam or cinnamon. The most highly prized perfume was imported from Arabia under the name of 'Scent of the Phoenix Nest'. Its composition was a closely guarded secret of the Arabian merchants and is now lost.

The tasteful decoration of the triclinium itself was considered vital. It was the most important room in the house, used for receiving visitors, entertaining guests and carrying out business. Even the poorest families would try to set aside a part of their apartments as a triclinium, although sometimes this meant simply erecting a cloth screen in one corner of a room. If no other room in the house had a mosaic, the triclinium did, and it was also graced with wall paintings. Those which have survived show that mythological scenes were popular for both floor mosaics and wall paintings. The quality of artwork in the houses of the richest men was exceptional, rivalling anything that modern artists can produce, but that was not enough. If a host wanted to make a really good impression, he would have the walls repainted with a new design for a particularly important event.

Even a relatively humble meal needed entertainment. This might involve a hired flute player coming in for an hour or so for a simple meal, or could be so elaborate as to involve dozens of performers and last all night. Hosts with fewer resources would hire in artistes, but the richer men prided themselves on buying highly skilled slaves to perform for their guests. Performances included the recitation of epic poems, the playing of popular songs and the reading of famous speeches from history.

At the saucier end of the scale were the dancing girls of Cadiz. Performing to the rhythmic beat of a drum and cymbals, the girls moved gracefully, but suggestively with much pouting of the breast and shaking of the bottom. Contrary to popular belief, there was a strict 'no touching' policy regarding the dancing girls. Their skill took years to learn and demanded constant practice and exercise and the fees they could command were high. A pregnancy would put them out of work for months.

A few hosts thoughtfully provided less skilled, but equally attractive waiting staff to titillate their guests. Most of these staff members were available for intimate conversations and fondling, but nothing more. Even at its most decadent, Roman society kept a clear demarcation between prostitutes and other staff. Some hosts did, of course, provide prostitutes, both female and male, for their guests, but such events were most unusual. Respectable Roman society preferred to keep such things to the brothels and taverns, not in their smart tricliniums.

Having arranged the food, scents, entertainment and decorations, it was time to invite the guests. A simple meal could be eaten with a few friends at relatively short notice. These meals traditionally had nine diners, including the host and his family. This was because the usual layout for a dining room was to have three couches, each able to hold three people, arranged around a central table on which the food was served. The couches had wooden frames supporting a web of leather straps over which were piled soft cushions. More upright chairs were sometimes provided for the elderly or for women.

More elaborate meals would also, at least officially, involve just nine diners. However, at formal meals it was usual for a visitor to bring along slaves to escort him through the streets in a manner fitting his status in life. These would need to be fed, usually in a side room off the kitchen.

There were also the clients to be considered. Clients were less wealthy Romans or those of a lower social standing who looked to a rich patron for business and other opportunities. In return he voted as the patron demanded, undertook favours or ran errands. When a formal dinner was given, the clients would expect to participate. They would not join the principal guests in the triclinium, but would dine in a nearby chamber. The more important clients would expect to feast on the same foods and wines as the main guests while less important clients would be served simpler dishes and cheaper wines. The main guests would also be expected to bring along their own clients to join in. A dinner which was in theory for nine people could end up with over a hundred diners.

Roman women and men commonly dined together, though it was not until Imperial times that women were welcome to join the men on the couches, instead of sitting on chairs. Women were expected to join in the conversations and to be as conversant with politics, literature or current affairs as the men. It was, however, unusual for unmarried women to attend formal dinners. It was considered rather improper for unmarried women to play a full role in society, though widows were free to do as they liked.

Rank and status were important at dinners. A host could invite his social inferiors to dine with him if he wished, but it was expected that all guests would be of approximately the same social rank. If a senator was invited to dine he would expect all the other guests to be from senatorial families. If he found himself rubbing shoulders with plebeians, he would consider the invitation to have been an insult no matter how grand the host might be. As today, putting together a guest list could be a social nightmare.

The frequency with which invitations and guest lists feature in Roman plays and writings indicates the importance of entertaining and dining to society. Hosts could make or ruin their reputations by inviting the wrong people, or not inviting the right ones, while guests could make fools of themselves by accepting invitations unworthy of their dignity in the social hierarchy.

Even when the invitations had been given and accepted there was room for social disaster. The guest of highest social rank reclined next to the host on the same couch, so there was the potential for choosing the wrong guest of honour. The remaining guests reclined around the table more or less at random, though at very formal meals some squabbling could take place over precedence.

Roman banquets could be debauched, refined or petty. Whatever form they took, they depended on a steady, secure supply of food. Roman government took great pains to ensure that this supply was maintained.

Queen Cleopatra of Egypt. The legendary beauty was seduced both by Julius Caesar and later his ally Mark Antony. After Antony's defeat by Octavian, Cleopatra famously chose to commit suicide with an asp, a poisonous snake, rather than be the star attraction of Octavian's Triumph in Rome.

IV

ˌ THE SEDUCTION OF ˌ
CLEOPATRA

THE POPULATION OF ROME grew as her empire increased. The demand for food imports rapidly became a crucial political issue in the Roman Republic and no politician who ignored it could expect a long career. In 241 BC Rome captured the fertile island of Sicily, ensuring a secure supply of grain and other consumables. The Roman demand for supplies to fill hungry mouths continued to grow and in 147 BC Rome captured Carthage and with it the vast wheatfields of North Africa, then at their most productive. Before long, however, Rome needed more and the Romans began to cast greedy eyes towards the greatest grain-producing country of the ancient world: Egypt.

Egypt had a history and culture stretching back 3,000 years, making Rome's 700 years seem almost insignificant. At the time the ancient kingdom was ruled by a Greek dynasty, known as the Ptolemies. Ptolemy I had been a general of Alexander the Great, who seized Egypt after his master's sudden death in 323 BC. The early Ptolemies brought Greek science to bear on the rich soil of Egypt. They introduced new varieties of crops, modern machinery and efficient administration. Within a generation the agricultural output of Egypt doubled, and with it her wealth.

The Ptolemies lavished their riches on the great library at Alexandria, on massive building projects and on creating the most civilized and cultured society of the ancient world. Gradually, however, the luxury and generations of inbreeding led to the decline of the dynasty. Incest and family violence came to be typical. In 80 BC Ptolemy X was killed by a rioting mob in Alexandria after news leaked out of the court that he had murdered his enormously popular wife and step-mother Berenice. The mob then raced to the home of an illegitimate son of Ptolemy VIII and offered him the throne of the pharaohs. The young man at once declared himself to be Ptolemy XI and moved into the royal palace to take possession of his vast and astonishingly wealthy inheritance.

Ptolemy XI, however, soon found he had a problem. An earlier treaty with Rome had stated that if the line of the Pharaohs died out, then the Republic of Rome would inherit Egypt. Ptolemy was illegitimate and some at Rome thought the treaty should be invoked and Egypt seized. Ptolemy hurried to Rome where he persuaded the Senate to recognize him as the legitimate sovereign of Egypt by distributing bribes so vast that even the corrupt Roman officials were amazed. Ptolemy won his vote, but he had given the unfortunate impression that Egypt was both wealthy and weak. Even more unfortunately for Egypt, the impression was only too true.

When Ptolemy died in 51 BC he left Egypt jointly to his daughter, Cleopatra, and her half-brother Ptolemy XII. The two married, but at once fell to bickering over how the nation should be governed. Civil war loomed. The Egyptians worried that their independence was once more under threat. At this point, Rome intervened again in the person of Julius Caesar.

Caesar had recently won a vicious civil war against his fellow Romans and came to Egypt to hunt down the fugitives. Although Ptolemy handed over to Caesar the bodies of his enemies, it was Cleopatra who captivated the Roman. Aged just twenty-one, Cleopatra set out to win over Caesar to her cause using political reality and her undoubted seductive charms. Forbidden access to Caesar by her brother-husband, Cleopatra asked permission to send him a gift of a carpet. When the carpet was unrolled in front of Caesar, the beautiful young queen tumbled out to lie at his feet.

Roman writers were as fascinated by Cleopatra as was Caesar. They claimed that she was not only beautiful, intelligent and artistic, but also trained in all the arts of sex and of love. The number of her lovers was no doubt exaggerated, but there can be no reason to doubt that she was an astonishingly captivating woman. She was also well-informed. She knew all about the dole of free grain handed out to Roman citizens and dangled before Caesar the promise of a steady supply from the vast production of Egypt.

Caesar was won over and used his army to crush the forces of Ptolemy XII and put Cleopatra on the throne as sole ruler. Cleopatra, in turn, gave Caesar a son who was named Ptolemy Caesarion. Cleopatra was secure on her throne, her kingdom was safely independent with an heir to the throne and she had the most powerful man in the known world as a supporter and lover. Then, in 44 BC, Caesar was murdered. Cleopatra's careful plans to safeguard herself and her kingdom fell into ruins.

The Roman empire became embroiled in civil war between the erstwhile supporters of Caesar and those who had assasinated him. The victors proved to be Caesar's nephew Octavian and his friend Mark Antony. The two men divided the empire between them, Octavian taking the western provinces and Antony the eastern lands. With his residence now in Cilicia, Antony received a visit from Cleopatra.

Cleopatra came to meet Antony at Tarsus. She was determined to gain the support of this new Roman ruler and left nothing to chance. She came in a magnificent vessel built to be a pleasure barge as much as a sea-going ship, and at the head of a fleet. The historian Plutarch recorded the scene:

> *The barge she sat in, like a polished throne, burned on the water. The poop was of beaten gold, the sails purple and so perfumed that the winds were love-sick for them. The oars were covered in solid silver and kept stroke to the tune of flutes. As for the Queen's own person, it defies description. She lay in a pavilion made of cloth of gold as if she were Venus and on each side of her stood pretty little boys, like cupids, with coloured fans whose wind seemed to glow on the delicate cheeks that they were cooling. Beautiful young women posed on the deck as the attendants to this goddess of love.*

The people of Tarsus rushed to the docks to watch the arrival, leaving Antony alone except for a few guards.

That evening Antony attended a banquet on the Egyptian barge.

Cleopatra laid on every luxury and delicacy that Egypt had to offer, and they were formidable. The room was awash with gold. Gold thread ran through the tapestries that hung on the walls and the upholstery of the dining couches. The plates and goblets were of solid gold, inlaid with precious stones. Musicians played while dancing girls performed. The meal itself was overwhelming. There were fish from the Nile and ducks from the swamps, dates from the desert and nuts from the Sudan. There was more exotic fruit than most Romans saw in a lifetime and the tables were piled with a bewildering array of vegetables, all prepared in the most tempting fashion. The light, delicate Egyptian wine from Mareotis and Saite flowed in vast quantities. And everywhere there was bread made from the very finest white flour to make the subtle political point about the importance of Egypt's crops in feeding Rome.

Antony was won over by the feast. When it ended, Cleopatra apologized to her guests that her cooks had not had time to prepare anything better. To make up for this supposed oversight, Cleopatra presented each diner with the gold plates and goblets they had been using.

Over the following days, Cleopatra introduced the rough soldier Antony to all the luxuries and culture of the East. She also talked serious politics, emphasising the wealth and splendour of Egypt and how it could be joined to the might of Rome to rule the world. Antony agreed to an alliance and began an affair with the Egyptian queen as had Caesar before him. They had three children, two boys and a girl, who joined Caesar's son in the royal nursery in Alexandria.

Together Antony and Cleopatra ran the wealthy lands of the eastern Mediterranean as a private empire. This did not go down well in Rome, whose provinces and cities Antony was effectively handing over to a foreign monarch. In the closing months of 31 BC Octavian went to war against Antony and Cleopatra. Within two years Octavian had his enemies under siege in Alexandria. Seeing no escape, Antony committed suicide.

Cleopatra stayed alive to try to negotiate with Octavian. She hoped to keep Egypt in her family, probably as a client state of Rome. But there was to be no deal with Octavian. His armies had crushed those of Egypt and he was in a position to take anything he wanted. What he wanted, was to take Cleopatra to Rome and march her in chains through the streets as part of his Triumph. Cleopatra would not accept such a fate.

She dressed herself in her finest ceremonial robes, arranged herself on a state couch in the palace and had herself bitten by a snake smuggled past the Roman guards.

Octavian respected Cleopatra's last wishes and buried her beside Antony. He then killed young Ptolemy Caesarion, Cleopatra's son by Caesar, who was handsome, talented and too close to the throne for comfort. Cleopatra's children by Antony were spared. The eldest, a girl named Selene, was married to Octavian's ally King Juba of Mauretania. Her two brothers were sent to live with her in that North African kingdom where they faded into quiet obscurity.

Egypt was unlike any other country captured by Octavian in the East. It was large, wealthy and ancient. He did not make it a province of the Roman Empire, which would have entailed its being put in the hands of a governor appointed by the Senate. Instead, Octavian had himself proclaimed as Pharaoh and ruler of Egypt. He appointed a general, Cornelius Gallus, whose loyalty could be trusted absolutely, to run Egypt on behalf of the new Pharaoh. Octavian then returned to Rome to be hailed as Augustus and to become the first Emperor.

As Pharaoh, Augustus had control of the vast wealth of the richest country in the known world. He used it to secure his position in Rome. He also had control of the grain supplies on which Rome depended. It was a potent political weapon. Augustus set about organizing it with typically Roman efficiency.

Replica of a Roman grain galley. The ever-increasing population of Rome could only be fed by importing vast amounts of grain from all over the Roman Empire. The grain fleets played a vital role in keeping Rome supplied.

V

' THE GRAIN FLEETS '

B Y 30 BC ROME HAD CONQUERED Sicily, North Africa and Egypt, the three great grain producing regions of the ancient world. The vast quantities of grain needed by Rome's million or so inhabitants could now be provided from within the Roman Empire. What was needed was an efficient system for getting the food from where it was grown to where it was consumed. The mighty grain fleets of the Empire were about to be born.

The grain had been shipped to Rome for centuries by private merchants using the usual trade routes and standard ships. These ships followed a fairly traditional pattern, one which had been found to be safe in Mediterranean waters and could be handled by a small crew, essential when costs had to be kept down to make a decent profit.

The size of these ships varied, but typically they could carry cargoes of between 150 and 300 tons. They were about seventy-five feet long and twenty feet in the beam, making them fairly tubby craft. The hull was built up of long planks fixed together by mortise and tenon joints, interior ribs were then fitted to add rigidity to the hull. The stern was rounded, sweeping up to end in a graceful, curved sternpost. The single deck ran right along the ship and the cargo was stored in the hull below. A small wooden or canvas cabin towards the rear provided shelter for the crew, and a small tiled hearth allowed a cooking fire to be lit with safety.

The ships had two masts, both of which carried a single square sail.

The main mast stood upright amidships and could be up to sixty feet tall. The foremast pointed forwards at an angle of about thirty degrees and was considerably smaller. The sail on the foremast seems to have been used chiefly to assist steering. There was no rudder, though a pair of steering oars at the rear made the ships fairly nimble. A modern replica of one of the smaller craft achieved speeds of about six knots and, although it could not sail into the wind, could get fairly close to it.

The sea routes used by these ships were determined by the habits of the seamen. Roman sailors did not like sailing at night. There were simply too many potential hazards and obstacles for it to be a sensible idea, so they anchored as dusk fell. Nor were they keen on sailing through storms, preferring to take shelter in a port if heavy seas were likely. This meant that ships tended to stay in coastal waters where seas were shallow enough for anchoring and ports could be found if bad weather threatened. Keeping within sight of the coast also made navigation easier as the master could follow landmarks to his destination.

The sea routes from Sicily were short and straightforward. From ports such as Syracuse, Messina and Agrigentum, the grains ships crossed the straits to Rhegium, then followed the west coast of Italy northward. The destination for these ships, and all others bringing food to Rome, was the port of Ostia near the mouth of the Tiber. If the winds were favourable, the journey from Sicily to Ostia could be completed in three or four days, though a northerly wind could keep ships in harbour for days on end.

At the height of its prosperity around AD 100, Ostia had a population of 90,000. The harbour was spacious and the docks lined by large warehouses able to store thousands of tons of grain. From Ostia the grain was taken up the Tiber on small lighters driven by oars to landing stages just down river of the city.

Ships sailing from North Africa would follow the coast to the city of Carthage, where a large harbour allowed them to shelter in considerable numbers awaiting southwesterly winds to make the day long sea crossing to the west coast of Sicily. From there the ships would follow the island coast to reach Rhegium and so sail on to Ostia.

The sea route from Egypt to Rome was far longer and more difficult. Ships could follow the African coast to Carthage before striking north.

This kept them within sight of land, but made the journey much longer than it would have been if the ships had sailed across the open seas. As a consequence, shipping Egyptian grain to Rome was expensive. Before 100 BC Rome called on Egyptian sources only in times of famine, when the pressing need made the long voyage worthwhile. After that date the growing population of Rome meant that Egyptian grain was a regular cargo to Rome. A small number of Roman and Egyptian masters became adept at making the long crossing over the open sea. By 50 BC they could complete their voyage in around seventeen days if the winds were favourable.

After Egypt was added to the Roman Empire in 30 BC the situation altered radically. As Pharaoh of Egypt, the Emperor of Rome found himself in ownership of the vast majority of the grain farming land. It made sense to transport this grain to Rome to provide the free dole that the Emperor was obliged to hand out to the poorer Roman citizens on a regular basis. At first, the grain was transported in ordinary ships by independent merchants. By about AD 50, however, the Imperial government was running the trade directly, using purpose-built craft.

The grain ships of Imperial Rome were among the wonders of the age. They were around 200 feet long and carried three masts. These enormous vessels could carry around 1,300 tons of grain in their capacious holds. So large were they that the docks at Alexandria and Ostia had to be completely rebuilt to be able to accommodate them. The Egyptian grain fleets sailed in the spring, as soon as the harvest had been gathered in and carried down the Nile to Alexandria. The fleets included dozens of grain ships, escorted by war galleys to deter pirates and keep an eye on the precious cargo.

For centuries Rome was fed by the merchant ships of Sicily and Africa and by the massive Egyptian grain ships, but the safe transportation of bulk grain cargoes relied heavily on Roman control of the Mediterranean. When Roman power began to fail in the later fourth century the safety of the sea routes came under threat. And that meant the food supply to Rome was in peril.

Successive attacks on Rome by the barbarians led to massive damage to the city and depopulation. During the siege of 538 the Romans converted the massively constructed walls of Hadrian's Tomb (above) into a powerful bastion which the Goths tried several times to capture, but which always held firm.

VI

، STARVATION AT ROME ،

I N THE YEAR 400 the city of Rome was large, rich and beautiful. The
streets were lined with marble temples and magnificent monuments.
The Forum was the heart of Empire with state temples and treasuries
jostling for space with the offices of the bureaucrats and the premises of
businessmen. The Colosseum saw frequent bloodthirsty games and the
Circus Maximus staged chariot races to keep the people entertained. At the
theatres were performed the finest dramas of the known world, while
more earthy comedies and mimes delighted the mobs. Free food was doled
out to the masses as a gift from the Emperor to the citizens of the greatest
city on Earth. The population was about 800,000 souls.

However, Rome was not as strong or as vibrant as it appeared. It was
no longer the powerhouse of the Empire. Instead of producing soldiers,
administrators and emperors, the city had become a vast, glorious and
beautiful sink of unemployment and dependence. The city relied upon
free food paid for by the Imperial government which taxed the provinces
to pay the bills. Few people in Rome worked at productive businesses.
They worked in what would today be called service industries to serve
each other, the money coming from the government or from rich men
who lived in the city and gained wealth from estates and investments
elsewhere. Nor was Rome the source of political power. The voting citizens had long become an irrelevance. Real might lay with the army whose
swords put emperors in position and kept them there.

Rome had become a magnificent irrelevance, but nobody realized it.

The emperors spent fortunes providing free food and free entertainments for the Roman mob. The Senate met to debate the issues of state. Above all the Romans themselves still believed their city was the centre of the world and blissfully believed their glory would be eternal.

On the edges of the Empire things did not seem so stable. The numbers and strength of the barbarian tribes beyond the frontiers was increasing steadily. Raids and wars were becoming more serious and more frequent. The army was increasingly manned by mercenaries hired from the barbarian tribes themselves and the diminishing proportion of 'Roman' troops in the armed forces were from the frontier provinces, not from Rome or even Italy. A series of plagues had reduced the population and economic troubles were causing the emperors to have problems raising and maintaining their armed forces.

In 378 the Emperor Valens and a large proportion of the Roman army was slaughtered by invading Goths at the Battle of Adrianople. The new Emperor Theodosius pushed the Goths back, but the Roman military had been weakened both materially and morally. When he died in 395, Theodosius made permanent the decades-old administrative division of the empire into East and West. He left the eastern half to one son, Arcadius, and the west to another son, Honorius. The two halves of the empire increasingly became quite separate states and followed different destinies.

Rome was robbed of the rich and populous cities of the East which for years had provided the taxes and wealth on which the city survived. Equally important, she was deprived of the vast grainfields of Egypt which had contributed the basic source of food for the people of Rome for over 400 years. The mighty city was now dependent on the wheat fields of Sicily, in serious decline due to soil erosion, and on supplies from North Africa.

In 402 the Goths led by their king Alaric invaded Italy, Under their general Stilicho, the Romans drove them back but suffered heavy casualties. No help had come to Honorius from his brother emperor in the East. Stilicho and Honorius withdrew troops from Britain and Gaul to make up the losses inflicted on the army in Italy. The seat of government was removed from Rome. The emperor and the imperial bureaucracy was installed in the easily defended fortress city of Ravenna. Rome had lost another facet of its might.

On the last day of the year 406 an alliance of three powerful Germanic tribes – the Vandals, Suebi and Alans – crossed the Rhine and attacked Gaul. The denuded Roman garrisons could do nothing to stop them. Within weeks most of northern Gaul was lost to the Roman Empire and Britain was isolated. Alaric and his Goths marched on Rome and only drew back when paid an immense bribe of 4,000 pounds of gold bullion. Stilicho was murdered in revenge for these military disasters and the Roman army was weakened even further as men loyal to their dead leader packed bags and went home.

In August 410 Alaric led his men to Rome. His army lacked siege weapons, but this was not immediately relevant as his first move was to seize Ostia and the grain warehouses. He hoped starvation would induce the Romans to pay him another bribe to leave, or that the Emperor Honorius in Ravenna would pay up. In the event a band of Goth slaves in the city opened the Salerian Gate and Alaric marched in. While his men looted houses of money, Alaric summoned the Senate and ordered them to strip all the moveable wealth from the temples and public buildings. When they read Alaric's list of required items the Senate was shocked. One exclaimed, 'Do you intend to leave anything in Rome?' Alaric grinned. 'Yes,' he replied. 'Your lives.'

The sack of Rome by Alaric and the Goths was a momentous event for the city. No foreign army had entered Rome for over eight centuries, now it seemed the barbarians could walk in when they pleased. After the Goths had gone thousands of people fled the city. Those with friends or relatives in the comparatively safe Eastern Empire hastened there, others went to North Africa.

Yet still Rome survived. Although gold, silver and money had been taken, the Goths had not burnt the city nor damaged the great public buildings. Within five years Rome looked much as it had done before Alaric arrived, though some houses and blocks of apartments were standing derelict due to the numbers of people who had fled. When Honorius led a Triumph through the streets in 415 he was greeted by vast crowds of cheering Romans and went on to mount a series of chariot races, animals fights and theatrical performances in the old monumental buildings. In 418 Honorius bought peace with the Goths by giving them Aquitaine to run as a semi-independent state within the Empire. The Vandals were settled on estates in southern Spain. Honorius regained control over plundered Gaul and re-established contact with Britain. Peace seemed to have returned and with it came people reoccupying Rome.

Then, in 427, disaster struck. Boniface, the governor of North Africa, announced that he was making his wealthy and fertile province independent of Rome and the Emperor Valentinian III, nephew of Honorius. Civil war erupted in North Africa. The chaos proved too much of a temptation for Gaiseric, King of the Vandals. Abandoning his status as a semi-independent ruler occupying estates in southern Spain, Gaiseric led his entire nation across the Straits of Gibraltar. Over the next ten years Gaiseric gradually conquered the rich and fertile lands of North Africa, fatally weakened by the rising of Boniface. In 439 he took Carthage. The Vandals now had absolute control over the food supply to Rome.

In 440 Gaiseric cut off the grain supply. Rome faced real starvation for the first time in centuries. Tens of thousands of people fled the city to seek food in other parts of the empire. In 442 Valentinian agreed a treaty with Gaiseric that restored the grain shipments in return for a heavy cash payment. This time, however, the citizens did not return to Rome as they had done after the sack of 410. The population was falling.

The beginning of the end for Rome as a great city came in 451. Attila the Hun, perhaps the greatest and most truly bloodthirsty barbarian of the era, called off his raids on the Eastern Empire and attacked Gaul. Valentinian and his general Aëtius marched the Roman army north and forged an alliance with the Goths, Burgundians and Alans. They defeated Attila at Chalons, but the Roman army now became an empty threat. The losses in manpower over the previous decades had been considerable as lands from which recruits might have come were lost to the barbarians. More serious was the loss of trained officers. The Roman soldiers were increasingly ill-disciplined and poorly trained. By the time it marched back to Italy after fighting Attila, the Roman army was little better than a barbarian army itself.

In 455 Emperor Valentinian III was murdered and amid mounting chaos and civil unrest, the Senate voted the wealthy nobleman Petronius Maximus to replace him. Gaiseric saw his chance. He used the fleet he had captured in North Africa to carry his army to Italy and laid siege to Rome. The new Emperor was promptly killed by his own citizens.

Gaiseric entered the city unopposed a few days later. He killed nobody, but stripped Rome, not only of money and plunder, but even of statues from the streets to take them to beautify his palace in Carthage. When Gaiseric pulled out, there was little left in Rome. The population was down to about half what it had been just forty years earlier.

The new power in Italy was Ricimer, commander of the shattered Roman army. This powerful barbarian mercenary chose a succession of compliant Romans to serve as Emperor. Significantly, Ricimer hardly ever bothered going to Rome to view the desolated city. In 472 Ricimer died, followed a few weeks later by his puppet the Emperor Olybrius. The Eastern Emperor sent a nobleman named Julius Nepos to take over the West, but in 475 he was driven back to the East by the new army commander Orestes.

The new strongman was a Roman from one of the oldest and wealthiest native families still in the city. In need of a new and compliant emperor he installed his own son. The 15-year-old boy was named Romulus, the name of the first King of Rome. He was then given the title of Augustus, that of the first Emperor of Rome. A year later Ricimer was stabbed to death during an argument with some of his German mercenary chiefs. The burly chieftains told young Romulus Augustus that he was no longer Emperor and sent him off to live on his family's estates south of Rome. The Germans carved Italy up into a series of kingdoms for themselves. The Roman Empire in the West was dead.

Rome appeared to be finished. There were few games to be celebrated and the bread dole had been discontinued after Gaiseric finally halted supplies of grain. After the abdication of the last Emperor in 476, Rome was no longer the capital of any state. It had no more reason to exist than did cities such as Milan or Ravenna. With luck it might have a future as a market town in the new barbarian kingdom of Italy.

But everything was not quite over. Rome was still a magical name rich with history and meaning. It was a prize worth fighting for. This was to prove unfortunate for the city. In 536 the Eastern Emperor sent an army under his general Belisarius to win Rome back for the Empire. Belisarius captured the city and at once was besieged by the Germans. The fighting dragged on for over a year, causing more damage to the buildings and reducing the population still further. When the Germans accepted defeat, Belisarius returned to Constantinople.

In 545 a new Goth king, Totila, rebelled against Constantinople. He marched straight on Rome, inflicting more damage and death on the dying city. In 552 a new general came from Constantinople. Narses defeated Totila, recaptured Rome and held a Triumph in the streets. The pavements of Rome were green with weeds, the buildings were collapsing and the aqueducts broken. Narses estimated that just 40,000 people lived in Rome where once there had been well over a million.

Narses died in Rome in 573 as a new wave of German barbarians, the Lombards, poured over the Alps. Six years later they laid siege to Rome, cutting off the food supply and destroying the repaired aqueducts. Famine stalked the city for months until the Lombards retreated. In 589 plague hit Rome, with starvation following quickly as farmers refused to enter the stricken city with food in case they caught the disease.

The once thronging population was down to barely 10,000. It seemed inevitable that Rome would go the way of Babylon, Ctesiphon and other capitals of fallen empires. It would soon be nothing but a tumble of empty ruins gradually decaying into dust.

But even as the old Rome died, a new Rome was about to be born. The Christian Bishops of Rome had for some years been claiming that they were superior to all other bishops. They asserted that they were the direct heirs to St Peter, himself appointed by Christ to lead the Church after the crucifixion. Even as the plague was raging a new Bishop of Rome was elected. This was Gregory I. He occupied the position of Pope for fourteen years. One of his first actions was to enforce Papal claims to extensive farming estates across central Italy. He hired workers and managers, making the land productive and ensuring the produce was brought to Rome so that famine was defeated. The action probably saved what was left of Rome's population.

Just as important, Gregory managed to assert the authority of the Pope over nearly all other Christian bishops and established the bureaucracy of the Christian religion in Rome. The city had a new reason to exist.

But despite the new future for the city, the past could not be brought back to life. The Rome of Bread and Circuses was dead and gone.

INDEX

Italic numbers refer to illustrations